Notetaker

PRINCIPLES OF MICROECONOMICS

Notetaker

PRINCIPLES OF MICROECONOMICS

Seventh Edition

Karl E. Case
Ray C. Fair

Fernando Quijano
Dickinson State University

PEARSON
Prentice
Hall

Upper Saddle River, New Jersey 07458

Editor-in-Chief: Jeff Shelstad
Executive Editor: David Alexander
Project Manager: Marie McHale
Manager, Print Production: Christy Mahon
Production Editor & Buyer: Wanda Rockwell
Printer/Binder: Bind-Rite Graphics

10 9 8 7 6 5 4 3 2 1
ISBN 0-13-185860-2

CHAPTER 1

**The Scope and
Method of Economics**

Prepared by: Fernando Quijano
and Yvonn Quijano

© 2004 Prentice Hall Business Publishing   Principles of Microeconomics, 7/e   Karl Case, Ray Fair

---

The Study of Economics

- *Economics* is the study of how individuals and societies choose to use the scarce resources that nature and previous generations have provided.

© 2004 Prentice Hall Business Publishing   Principles of Microeconomics, 7/e   Karl Case, Ray Fair

---

Why Study Economics?

- An important reason for studying economics is *to learn a way of thinking.*

- Three fundamental concepts:

  - *Opportunity cost*

  - *Marginalism*, and

  - *Efficient markets*

© 2004 Prentice Hall Business Publishing   Principles of Microeconomics, 7/e   Karl Case, Ray Fair

Opportunity Cost

- **Opportunity cost** is the best alternative that we forgo, or give up, when we make a choice or a decision.

- Nearly all decisions involve trade-offs.

Marginalism

- In weighing the costs and benefits of a decision, it is important to weigh only the costs and benefits that arise from the decision.

Marginalism

- For example, when a firm decides whether to produce additional output, it considers only the **additional** (or marginal cost), not the sunk cost.

  - **Sunk costs** are costs that cannot be avoided, regardless of what is done in the future, because they have already been incurred.

Efficient Markets

- An *efficient market* is one in which profit opportunities are eliminated almost instantaneously.

- There is no free lunch! Profit opportunities are rare because, at any one time, there are many people searching for them.

More Reasons to Study Economics

- The study of economics is an essential part of the study of society.

- Economic decisions often have enormous consequences.

  - During the *Industrial Revolution*, new manufacturing technologies and improved transportation gave rise to the modern factory system.

More Reasons to Study Economics

- An understanding of economics is essential to an understanding of global affairs.

- Voting decisions also require a basic understanding of economics.

The Scope of Economics

- *Microeconomics* is the branch of economics that examines the behavior of individual decision-making units—that is, business firms and households.

The Scope of Economics

- *Macroeconomics* is the branch of economics that examines the behavior of *economic aggregates*— income, output, employment, and so on— on a national scale.

The Scope of Economics

Examples of microeconomic and macroeconomic concerns

	Production	Prices	Income	Employment
Microeconomics	Production/Output in Individual Industries and Businesses How much steel How many offices How many cars	Price of Individual Goods and Services Price of medical care Price of gasoline Food prices Apartment rents	Distribution of Income and Wealth Wages in the auto industry Minimum wages Executive salaries Poverty	Employment by Individual Businesses & Industries Jobs in the steel industry Number of employees in a firm
Macroeconomics	National Production/Output Total Industrial Output Gross Domestic Product Growth of Output	Aggregate Price Level Consumer prices Producer Prices Rate of Inflation	National Income Total wages and salaries Total corporate profits	Employment and Unemployment in the Economy Total number of jobs Unemployment rate

The Method of Economics

- *Positive economics* studies economic behavior without making judgments. It describes what exists and how it works.

The Method of Economics

- *Normative economics*, also called policy economics, analyzes outcomes of economic behavior, evaluates them as good or bad, and may prescribe courses of action.

The Method of Economics

- *Positive economics* includes:
  - *Descriptive economics*, which involves the compilation of data that describe phenomena and facts.
  - *Economic theory,* which involves building models of behavior.
    - An *economic theory* is a general statement of cause and effect, action and reaction.

Theories and Models

- Theories involve models, and models involve variables.
- A *model* is a formal statement of a theory. Models are descriptions of the relationship between two or more variables.

Theories and Models

- **Ockham's razor** is the principle that irrelevant detail should be cut away. Models are simplifications, not complications, of reality.

Theories and Models

- A **variable** is a measure that can change from observation to observation.
- The *ceteris paribus* device is part of the process of abstraction.
  - Using the *ceteris paribus*, or *all else equal, assumption*, economists study the relationship between two variables while the values of other variables remain constant.

Theories and Models

- Pitfalls to avoid in formulating economic theory:

  - The *post hoc, ergo propter hoc fallacy* refers to a common error made in thinking about causation: If event A happened before event B, it is not necessarily true that A caused B.

  - The *fallacy of composition* is the erroneous belief that what is true for a part is also true for the whole.

The Method of Economics

- *Empirical economics* refers to the collection and use of data to test economic theories.

- Many data sets are available to facilitate economic research. They are collected by both government agencies and private companies,

Economic Policy

Criteria for judging economic outcomes:

- *Efficiency*, or allocative efficiency. An efficient economy is one that produces what people want at the least possible cost.

- *Equity*, or fairness of economic outcomes.

Economic Policy

Criteria for judging economic outcomes:

- ***Economic growth***, or an increase in the total output of an economy.
- ***Economic stability***, or the condition in which output is steady or growing, with low inflation and full employment of resources.

© 2004 Prentice Hall Business Publishing Principles of Microeconomics, 7/e Karl Case, Ray Fair

Review Terms and Concepts

ceteris paribus	macroeconomics
descriptive economics	microeconomics
economic growth	model
economic theory	normative economics
economics	Ockham's razor
efficiency	opportunity cost
efficient market	positive economics
empirical economics	post hoc, ergo propter hoc
equity	stability
fallacy of composition	sunk costs
Industrial Revolution	variable

© 2004 Prentice Hall Business Publishing Principles of Microeconomics, 7/e Karl Case, Ray Fair

Appendix: How to Read and Understand Graphs

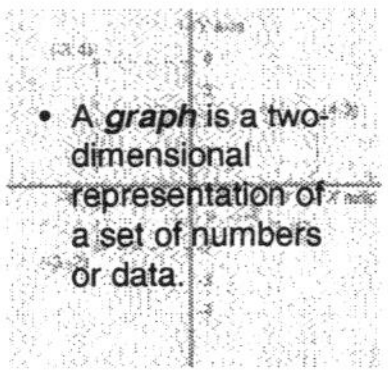

- A ***graph*** is a two-dimensional representation of a set of numbers or data.

© 2004 Prentice Hall Business Publishing Principles of Microeconomics, 7/e Karl Case, Ray Fair

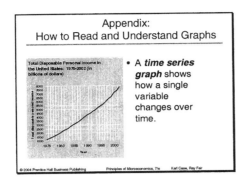

Appendix:
How to Read and Understand Graphs

- A *time series graph* shows how a single variable changes over time.

_____

_____

_____

_____

_____

_____

_____

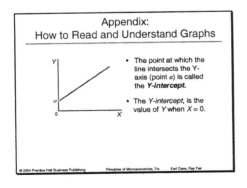

Appendix:
How to Read and Understand Graphs

- The *Cartesian coordinate system* is the most common method of showing the relationship between two variables.
- The horizontal line is the *X-axis* and the vertical line the *Y-axis*. The point at which the horizontal and vertical axes intersect is called the *origin*.

_____

_____

_____

_____

_____

_____

_____

Appendix:
How to Read and Understand Graphs

- The point at which the line intersects the Y-axis (point *a*) is called the *Y-intercept*.
- The *Y-intercept*, is the value of *Y* when *X* = 0.

_____

_____

_____

_____

_____

_____

_____

Appendix:
How to Read and Understand Graphs

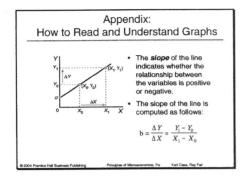

- The *slope* of the line indicates whether the relationship between the variables is positive or negative.

- The slope of the line is computed as follows:

$$b = \frac{\Delta Y}{\Delta X} = \frac{Y_1 - Y_0}{X_1 - X_0}$$

Appendix:
How to Read and Understand Graphs

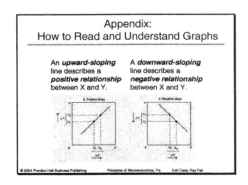

- This line slopes upward, indicating that there seems to be a positive relationship between income and spending.

- Points *A* and *B*, above the 45° line, show that consumption can be greater than income.

Appendix:
How to Read and Understand Graphs

An *upward-sloping* line describes a *positive relationship* between X and Y.

A *downward-sloping* line describes a *negative relationship* between X and Y.

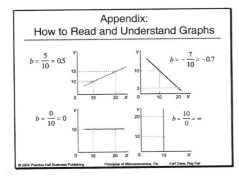

Appendix:
How to Read and Understand Graphs

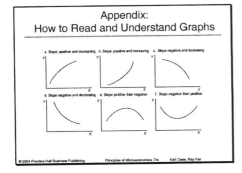

Appendix:
How to Read and Understand Graphs

Appendix:
How to Read and Understand Graphs

Cartesian coordinate system   slope
graph   time series graph
negative relationship   X-axis
origin   Y-axis
positive relationship   Y-intercept

CHAPTER 2

The Economic Problem:
Scarcity and Choice

Prepared by: Fernando Quijano
and Yvonn Quijano

© 2004 Prentice Hall Business Publishing   Principles of Microeconomics, 7/e   Karl Case, Ray Fair

---

Scarcity, Choice, and Opportunity Cost

- *Human wants are unlimited, but resources are not.*

- Three basic questions must be answered in order to understand an economic system:

  - What gets produced?

  - How is it produced?

  - Who gets what is produced?

© 2004 Prentice Hall Business Publishing   Principles of Microeconomics, 7/e   Karl Case, Ray Fair

---

Scarcity, Choice, and Opportunity Cost

The three basic questions:

1. What gets produced?   2. How is it produced?   3. Who gets what is produced?

Mix of output

Resources   Producers   Households

Allocation of resources   Distribution of output

- Every society has some system or mechanism that transforms that society's scarce resources into useful goods and services.

© 2004 Prentice Hall Business Publishing   Principles of Microeconomics, 7/e   Karl Case, Ray Fair

Scarcity, Choice, and Opportunity Cost

- *Capital* refers to the things that are themselves produced and then used to produce other goods and services.

- The basic resources that are available to a society are *factors of production*:
  - *Land*
  - *Labor*
  - *Capital*

© 2004 Prentice Hall Business Publishing   Principles of Microeconomics, 7/e   Karl Case, Ray Fair

Scarcity, Choice, and Opportunity Cost

- *Production* is the process that transforms scarce resources into useful goods and services.

- Resources or factors of production are the *inputs* into the process of production; goods and services of value to households are the *outputs* of the process of production.

© 2004 Prentice Hall Business Publishing   Principles of Microeconomics, 7/e   Karl Case, Ray Fair

Scarcity and Choice in a One-Person Economy

- Nearly all the basic decisions that characterize complex economies must also be made in a single-person economy.

- *Constrained choice* and *scarcity* are the basic concepts that apply to every society.

© 2004 Prentice Hall Business Publishing   Principles of Microeconomics, 7/e   Karl Case, Ray Fair

Scarcity and Choice in a One-Person Economy

- *Opportunity cost* is that which we give up or forgo, when we make a decision or a choice.

© 2004 Prentice Hall Business Publishing   Principles of Microeconomics, 7/e   Karl Case, Ray Fair

Scarcity and Choice in an Economy of Two or More

- A producer has an *absolute advantage* over another in the production of a good or service if it can produce that product using fewer resources.

© 2004 Prentice Hall Business Publishing   Principles of Microeconomics, 7/e   Karl Case, Ray Fair

Scarcity and Choice in an Economy of Two or More

- A producer has a *comparative advantage* in the production of a good or service over another if it can produce that product at a lower opportunity cost.

© 2004 Prentice Hall Business Publishing   Principles of Microeconomics, 7/e   Karl Case, Ray Fair

Comparative Advantage and the Gains From Trade

	Daily Production	
	Wood (logs)	Food (bushels)
Colleen	10	10
Bill	4	8

- Colleen has an *absolute advantage* in the production of both wood and food because she can produce more of both goods using fewer resources than Bill.

Comparative Advantage and the Gains From Trade

	Daily Production	
	Wood (logs)	Food (bushels)
Colleen	10	10
Bill	4	8

- **In terms of wood:**
  - For Bill, the opportunity cost of 8 bushels of food is 4 logs.
  - For Colleen, the opportunity cost of 8 bushels of food is 8 logs.
- **In terms of food:**
  - For Colleen, the opportunity cost of 10 logs is 10 bushels of food.
  - For Bill, the opportunity cost of 10 logs is 20 bushels of food.

Comparative Advantage and the Gains From Trade

- Suppose that Colleen and Bill each wanted equal numbers of logs and bushels of food. In a 30-day month they (each separately) could produce:

	Daily Production	
	Wood (logs)	Food (bushels)
Colleen	10	10
Bill	4	8

A.

	Monthly Production with No Trade	
	Wood (logs)	Food (bushels)
Colleen		
Bill		
Total		

B.

Comparative Advantage and the Gains From Trade

- By specializing on the basis of comparative advantage, Colleen and Bill can produce more of both goods.

	Monthly Production with No Trade		
	Wood (logs)	Food (bushels)
Colleen	150	150
Bill	80	80
Total	230	230

B.

	Monthly Production after Specialization		
	Wood (logs)	Food (bushels)
Colleen	270	30
Bill	0	240
Total	270	270

C.

Comparative Advantage and the Gains From Trade

- To end up with equal amounts of wood and food after trade, Colleen could trade 100 logs for 140 bushels of food. Then:

	Monthly Production after Specialization		
	Wood (logs)	Food (bushels)
Colleen	270	30
Bill	0	240
Total	270	270

C.

	Monthly Use After Trade		
	Wood (logs)	Food (bushels)
Colleen	170	170
Bill	100	100
Total	270	270

D.

Specialization, Exchange and Comparative Advantage

- According to the *theory of comparative advantage,* specialization and free trade will benefit all trading parties, even those that may be absolutely more efficient producers.

Capital Goods and Consumer Goods

- *Capital goods* are goods used to produce other goods and services.
- *Consumer goods* are goods produced for present consumption.

© 2004 Prentice Hall Business Publishing   Principles of Microeconomics, 7/e   Karl Case, Ray Fair

Capital Goods and Consumer Goods

- *Investment* is the process of using resources to produce new capital. Capital is the accumulation of previous investment.
- The opportunity cost of every investment in capital is forgone present consumption.

© 2004 Prentice Hall Business Publishing   Principles of Microeconomics, 7/e   Karl Case, Ray Fair

The Production Possibility Frontier

- The *production possibility frontier (ppf)* is a graph that shows all of the combinations of goods and services that can be produced if all of society's resources are used efficiently.

© 2004 Prentice Hall Business Publishing   Principles of Microeconomics, 7/e   Karl Case, Ray Fair

The Production Possibility Frontier

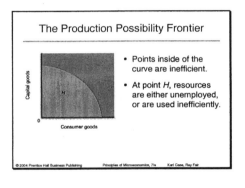

- The production possibility frontier curve has a negative slope, which indicates a trade-off between producing one good or another.

© 2004 Prentice Hall Business Publishing   Principles of Microeconomics, 7/e   Karl Case, Ray Fair

The Production Possibility Frontier

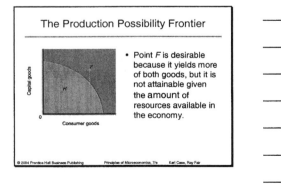

- Points inside of the curve are inefficient.
- At point *H*, resources are either unemployed, or are used inefficiently.

© 2004 Prentice Hall Business Publishing   Principles of Microeconomics, 7/e   Karl Case, Ray Fair

The Production Possibility Frontier

- Point *F* is desirable because it yields more of both goods, but it is not attainable given the amount of resources available in the economy.

© 2004 Prentice Hall Business Publishing   Principles of Microeconomics, 7/e   Karl Case, Ray Fair

The Production Possibility Frontier

- Point *C* is one of the possible combinations of goods produced when resources are fully and efficiently employed.

The Production Possibility Frontier

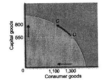

- A move along the curve illustrates the concept of opportunity cost.

- From point D, an increase the production of capital goods requires a decrease in the amount of consumer goods.

The Law of Increasing Opportunity Cost

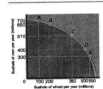

- The slope of the ppf curve is also called the *marginal rate of transformation (MRT)*.

- The negative slope of the ppf curve reflects the *law of increasing opportunity cost*. As we increase the production of one good, we sacrifice progressively more of the other.

Economic Growth

- *Economic growth* is an increase in the total output of the economy. It occurs when a society acquires new resources, or when it learns to produce more using existing resources.

- The main sources of economic growth are capital accumulation and technological advances.

Economic Growth

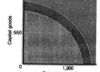

- Outward shifts of the curve represent *economic growth.*

- An outward shift means that it is possible to increase the production of one good without decreasing the production of the other.

Economic Growth

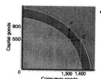

- From point D, the economy can choose any combination of output between F and G.

Economic Growth

- Not every sector of the economy grows at the same rate.

- In this historic example, productivity increases were more dramatic for corn than for wheat over this time period.

© 2004 Prentice Hall Business Publishing   Principles of Microeconomics, 7/e   Karl Case, Ray Fair

Capital Goods and Growth in Poor and Rich Countries

- Rich countries devote more resources to capital production than poor countries.

- As more resources flow into capital production, the rate of economic growth in rich countries increases, and so does the gap between rich and poor countries.

© 2004 Prentice Hall Business Publishing   Principles of Microeconomics, 7/e   Karl Case, Ray Fair

Economic Growth and the Gains From Trade

- By specializing and engaging in trade, Colleen and Bill can move beyond their own production possibilities.

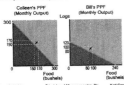

© 2004 Prentice Hall Business Publishing   Principles of Microeconomics, 7/e   Karl Case, Ray Fair

Economic Systems

- **The economic problem:**
  Given scarce resources, how, exactly, do large, complex societies go about answering the three basic economic questions?

Economic Systems

- *Economic systems* are the basic arrangements made by societies to solve the economic problem. They include:

  - Command economies

  - Laissez-faire economies

  - Mixed systems

Economic Systems

- In a *command economy*, a central government either directly or indirectly sets output targets, incomes, and prices.

- In a *laissez-faire economy*, individuals and firms pursue their own self-interests without any central direction or regulation.

Economic Systems

- The central institution of a laissez-faire economy is the *free-market system*.
- A **market** is the institution through which buyers and sellers interact and engage in exchange.

Economic Systems

- *Consumer sovereignty* is the idea that consumers ultimately dictate what will be produced (or not produced) by choosing what to purchase (and what not to purchase).

Economic Systems

- *Free enterprise:* under a free market system, individual producers must figure out how to plan, organize, and coordinate the production of products and services.

Economic Systems

- In a laissez-faire economy, the *distribution of output* is also determined in a decentralized way. The amount that any one household gets depends on its income and wealth.

Economic Systems

- The basic coordinating mechanism in a free market system is price. *Price* is the amount that a product sells for per unit. It reflects what society is willing to pay.

Mixed Systems, Markets, and Governments

Since markets are not perfect, governments intervene and often play a major role in the economy. Some of the goals of government are to:

- Minimize market inefficiencies
- Provide public goods
- Redistribute income
- Stabilize the macroeconomy:
  - Promote low levels of unemployment
  - Promote low levels of inflation

Review Terms and Concepts

absolute advantage	laissez-faire economy
capital	marginal rate of transformation (mrt)
command economy	market
comparative advantage, theory of	opportunity cost
consumer goods	outputs
consumer sovereignty	price
economic growth	production
economic problem	production possibility frontier (ppf)
investment	resources or inputs
	three basic questions

© 2004 Prentice Hall Business Publishing   Principles of Microeconomics, 7/e   Karl Case, Ray Fair

---

CHAPTER

3

Demand, Supply, and Market Equilibrium

Prepared by: Fernando Quijano
and Yvonn Quijano

© 2004 Prentice Hall Business Publishing   Principles of Microeconomics, 7/e   Karl Case, Ray Fair

---

Firms and Households: The Basic Decision-Making Units

- A **firm** is an organization that transforms resources (inputs) into products (outputs). Firms are the primary producing units in a market economy.

- An **entrepreneur** is a person who organizes, manages, and assumes the risks of a firm, taking a new idea or a new product and turning it into a successful business.

- **Households** are the consuming units in an economy.

© 2004 Prentice Hall Business Publishing   Principles of Microeconomics, 7/e   Karl Case, Ray Fair

Input Markets and Output Markets: The Circular Flow

- The *circular flow of economic activity* shows how firms and households interact in input and output markets.

Input Markets and Output Markets: The Circular Flow

- *Product* or *output markets* are the markets in which goods and services are exchanged.

- *Input markets* are the markets in which resources—labor, capital, and land—used to produce products, are exchanged.

Input Markets and Output Markets: The Circular Flow

- Goods and services flow clockwise. Firms provide goods and services; households supply labor services.

- Payments (usually money) flow in the opposite direction (counterclockwise) as the flow of labor services, goods, and services.

Input Markets and Output Markets:
The Circular Flow

- *Input* or *factor markets* are the markets in which the resources used to produce products are exchanged. They include:
  - The *labor market*, in which households supply work for wages to firms that demand labor.

Input Markets and Output Markets:
The Circular Flow

- *Input* or *factor markets* are the markets in which the resources used to produce products are exchanged. They include:
  - The *capital market*, in which households supply their savings, for interest or for claims to future profits, to firms that demand funds to buy capital goods.

Input Markets and Output Markets:
The Circular Flow

- *Input* or *factor markets* are the markets in which the resources used to produce products are exchanged. They include:
  - The *land market*, in which households supply land or other real property in exchange for rent.

Input Markets and Output Markets: The Circular Flow

- Inputs into the production process are also called *factors of production.*

Demand in Product/Output Markets

- A household's decision about the quantity of a particular output to demand depends on:
  - The *price of the product* in question.
  - The *income* available to the household.

Demand in Product/Output Markets

- A household's decision about the quantity of a particular output to demand depends on:
  - The household's amount of *accumulated wealth.*
  - The *prices of other products* (substitutes and complements) available to the household.

Demand in Product/Output Markets

- A household's decision about the quantity of a particular output to demand depends on:
  - The household's *tastes and preferences*.
  - The household's *expectations* about future income, wealth, and prices.

Demand in Product/Output Markets

- *Quantity demanded* is the amount (number of units) of a product that a household would buy in a given time period if it could buy all it wanted at the current market price.

Changes in Quantity Demanded Versus Changes in Demand

- The most important relationship in individual markets is that between market price and quantity demanded.

Changes in Quantity Demanded Versus Changes in Demand

- We use the *ceteris paribus* or "all else equal" device, to examine the relationship between the quantity demanded of a good per period of time and the price of that good, while holding income, wealth, other prices, tastes, and expectations constant.

Changes in Quantity Demanded Versus Changes in Demand

- Changes in price affect the *quantity demanded* per period.

- Changes in income, wealth, other prices, tastes, or expectations affect *demand*.

Price and Quantity Demanded: The Law of Demand

- A *demand schedule* is a table showing how much of a given product a household would be willing to buy at different prices.

- Demand curves are usually derived from demand schedules.

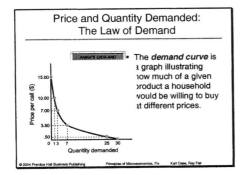

Price and Quantity Demanded: The Law of Demand

• The *demand curve* is a graph illustrating how much of a given product a household would be willing to buy at different prices.

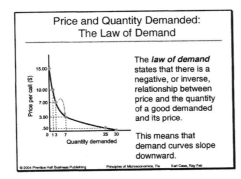

Price and Quantity Demanded: The Law of Demand

The *law of demand* states that there is a negative, or inverse, relationship between price and the quantity of a good demanded and its price.

This means that demand curves slope downward.

Other Determinants of Household Demand

• *Income* is the sum of all households wages, salaries, profits, interest payments, rents, and other forms of earnings in a given period of time. It is a *flow* measure.

• *Wealth*, or *net worth*, is the total value of what a household owns minus what it owes. It is a *stock* measure.

Other Determinants of Household Demand

- *Normal Goods* are goods for which demand goes up when income is higher and for which demand goes down when income is lower.
- *Inferior Goods* are goods for which demand falls when income rises.

Other Determinants of Household Demand

- *Substitutes* are goods that can serve as replacements for one another; when the price of one increases, demand for the other goes up.
- *Perfect substitutes* are identical products.

Other Determinants of Household Demand

- *Complements* are goods that "go together"; a decrease in the price of one results in an increase in demand for the other, and vice versa.

Shift of Demand Versus Movement Along a Demand Curve

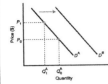

A change in *demand* is not the same as a change in *quantity demanded*.

A higher price causes lower *quantity demanded* and a move along the demand curve D_A.

Changes in determinants of demand, other than price, cause a change in *demand*, or a *shift* of the entire demand curve, from D_A to D_B.

© 2004 Prentice Hall Business Publishing   Principles of Microeconomics, 7/e   Karl Case, Ray Fair

---

A Change in Demand Versus a Change in Quantity Demanded

To summarize:

Change in price of a good or service leads to

  Change in *quantity demanded* (**Movement along the curve**).

Change in income, preferences, or prices of other goods or services leads to

  Change in demand (**Shift of curve**).

© 2004 Prentice Hall Business Publishing   Principles of Microeconomics, 7/e   Karl Case, Ray Fair

---

The Impact of a Change in Income

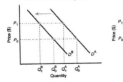
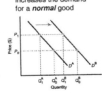

- Higher income decreases the demand for an *inferior* good

- Higher income increases the demand for a *normal* good

© 2004 Prentice Hall Business Publishing   Principles of Microeconomics, 7/e   Karl Case, Ray Fair

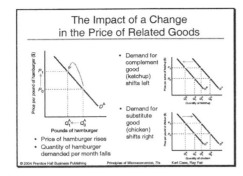

The Impact of a Change in the Price of Related Goods

- Price of hamburger rises
- Quantity of hamburger demanded per month falls
- Demand for complement good (ketchup) shifts left
- Demand for substitute good (chicken) shifts right

From Household Demand to Market Demand

- Demand for a good or service can be defined for an *individual household*, or for a group of households that make up a *market*.

- *Market demand* is the sum of all the quantities of a good or service demanded per period by all the households buying in the market for that good or service.

From Household Demand to Market Demand

- Assuming there are only two households in the market, market demand is derived as follows:

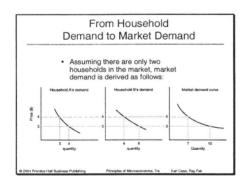

Supply in Product/Output Markets

- Supply decisions depend on profit potential.
- *Profit* is the difference between revenues and costs.

Supply in Product/Output Markets

- *Quantity supplied* represents the number of units of a product that a firm would be willing and able to offer for sale at a particular price during a given time period.
- A *supply schedule* is a table showing how much of a product firms will supply at different prices.

Price and Quantity Supplied: The Law of Supply

- A *supply curve* is a graph illustrating how much of a product a firm will supply per period of time at different prices.

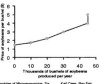

Price and Quantity Supplied: The Law of Supply

- The *law of supply* states that there is a positive relationship between price and quantity of a good supplied.
- This means that supply curves typically have a positive slope.

© 2004 Prentice Hall Business Publishing   Principles of Microeconomics, 7/e   Karl Case, Ray Fair

Other Determinants of Supply

- The *price* of the good or service.
- The *cost* of producing the good, which in turn depends on:
  - The *price of required inputs* (labor, capital, and land),
  - The *technologies* that can be used to produce the product,
- The *prices of related products.*

© 2004 Prentice Hall Business Publishing   Principles of Microeconomics, 7/e   Karl Case, Ray Fair

Shift of Supply Versus Movement Along a Supply Curve

- A higher price causes *higher quantity supplied*, and a *move along* the demand curve.

A change in determinants of supply other than price causes an *increase in supply*, or a *shift* of the entire supply curve, from S_A to S_B.

© 2004 Prentice Hall Business Publishing   Principles of Microeconomics, 7/e   Karl Case, Ray Fair

Shift of Supply Curve for Soybeans Following Development of a New Seed Strain

- In this example, since the factor affecting supply is not the price of soybeans but a technological change in soybean production, there is a shift of the supply curve rather than a movement along the supply curve.

- The technological advance means that more output can be supplied for at any given price level.

Shift of Supply Versus Movement Along a Supply Curve

To summarize:

Change in price of a good or service leads to

→ Change in *quantity supplied* (**Movement along the curve**).

Change in costs, input prices, technology, or prices of related goods and services leads to

→ Change in supply (**Shift of curve**).

From Individual Supply to Market Supply

- The supply of a good or service can be defined for an individual firm, or for a group of firms that make up a market or an industry.

- *Market supply* is the sum of all the quantities of a good or service supplied per period by all the firms selling in the market for that good or service.

From Individual Supply to Market Supply

- As with market demand, **market supply** is the horizontal summation of individual firms' supply curves.

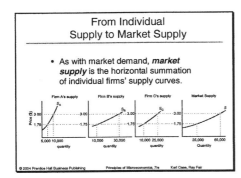

Market Equilibrium

- **Market equilibrium** is the condition that exists when quantity supplied and quantity demanded are equal.

- At equilibrium, there is no tendency for the market price to change.

Market Equilibrium

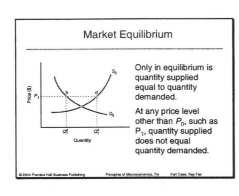

Only in equilibrium is quantity supplied equal to quantity demanded.

At any price level other than P_0, such as P_1, quantity supplied does not equal quantity demanded.

Excess Demand

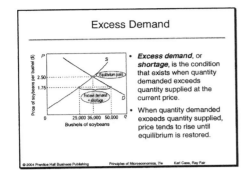

- **Excess demand**, or **shortage**, is the condition that exists when quantity demanded exceeds quantity supplied at the current price.
- When quantity demanded exceeds quantity supplied, price tends to rise until equilibrium is restored.

© 2004 Prentice Hall Business Publishing   Principles of Microeconomics, 7/e   Karl Case, Ray Fair

Excess Supply

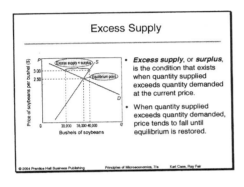

- **Excess supply**, or **surplus**, is the condition that exists when quantity supplied exceeds quantity demanded at the current price.
- When quantity supplied exceeds quantity demanded, price tends to fall until equilibrium is restored.

© 2004 Prentice Hall Business Publishing   Principles of Microeconomics, 7/e   Karl Case, Ray Fair

Changes in Equilibrium

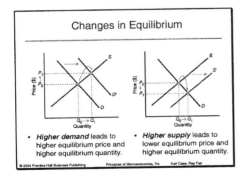

- **Higher demand** leads to higher equilibrium price and higher equilibrium quantity.
- **Higher supply** leads to lower equilibrium price and higher equilibrium quantity.

© 2004 Prentice Hall Business Publishing   Principles of Microeconomics, 7/e   Karl Case, Ray Fair

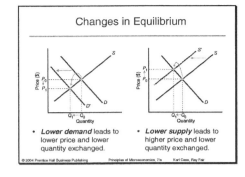

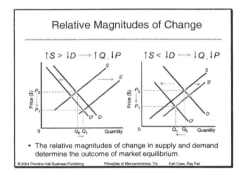

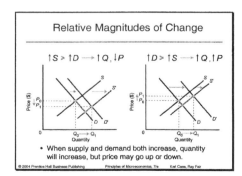

Review Terms and Concepts

capital market
commitments,
   complementary goods
demand curve
demand schedule
entrepreneur
equilibrium
excess demand or shortage
excess supply or surplus
factors of production
firm
households

income
inputs goods
main or factor markets
labor market
land market
law of demand
law of supply
market demand
market supply
movements along a
   demand curve
normal goods

perfect substitutes
product or output markets
profit
quantity demanded
quantity supplied
shift of a demand curve
substitutes
supply curve
supply schedule
wealth or net worth

CHAPTER 4

Demand and Supply
Applications and Elasticity

Prepared by: Fernando Quijano
and Yvonn Quijano

The Price System:
Rationing and Allocating Resources

- The market system, performs two important and closely related functions:

  1. **Resource allocation:** the market system determines the allocation of resources among produces and the final mix of outputs.

The Price System: Rationing and Allocating Resources

- The market system, performs two important and closely related functions:

  2. **Price rationing:** the market system distributes goods and services on the basis of willingness and ability to pay.

Price Rationing

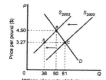

- A decrease in supply creates a shortage at the original price.

- The lower supply is rationed to those who are willing and able to pay the higher price.

Price Rationing

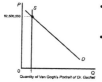

- There is some price that will clear any market.

- The price of a rare painting will eliminate excess demand until there is only one bidder willing to buy the single available painting.

Constraints on the Market

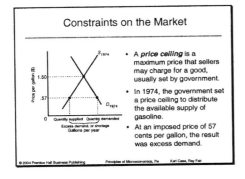

- A *price ceiling* is a maximum price that sellers may charge for a good, usually set by government.
- In 1974, the government set a price ceiling to distribute the available supply of gasoline.
- At an imposed price of 57 cents per gallon, the result was excess demand.

© 2004 Prentice Hall Business Publishing   Principles of Microeconomics, 7/e   Karl Case, Ray Fair

---

Alternative Rationing Mechanisms

- *Queuing* is a nonprice rationing system that uses waiting in line as a means of distributing goods and services.

© 2004 Prentice Hall Business Publishing   Principles of Microeconomics, 7/e   Karl Case, Ray Fair

---

Alternative Rationing Mechanisms

- *Favored customers* are those who receive special treatment from dealers during situations when there is excess demand.
- *Ration coupons* are tickets or coupons that entitle individuals to purchase a certain amount of a given product per month.

© 2004 Prentice Hall Business Publishing   Principles of Microeconomics, 7/e   Karl Case, Ray Fair

Alternative Rationing Mechanisms

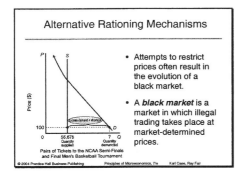

Pairs of Tickets to the NCAA Semi-Finals
and Final Men's Basketball Tournament

- Attempts to restrict prices often result in the evolution of a black market.

- A *black market* is a market in which illegal trading takes place at market-determined prices.

© 2004 Prentice Hall Business Publishing   Principles of Microeconomics, 7/e   Karl Case, Ray Fair

Alternative Rationing Mechanisms

- The problem with rationing systems is that excess demand is created but not eliminated.

- No matter how good the intentions of private organizations and governments, it is very difficult to prevent the price system from operating and to stop the willingness to pay from asserting itself.

© 2004 Prentice Hall Business Publishing   Principles of Microeconomics, 7/e   Karl Case, Ray Fair

Prices and the Allocation of Resources

- Price changes resulting from shifts of demand cause profits to rise or fall.

- Profits attract capital; losses lead to disinvestment.

- Higher wages attract labor and encourage workers to acquire skills.

- At the core of the system, supply, demand, and prices in input and output markets determine the allocation of resources and the ultimate combinations of things produced.

© 2004 Prentice Hall Business Publishing   Principles of Microeconomics, 7/e   Karl Case, Ray Fair

---

Price Floors

- A **price floor** is a minimum price below which exchange is not permitted.
  - The most common example of a price floor is the **minimum wage**, which is a floor set under the price of labor.
- The result of setting a price floor will be excess supply, or higher quantity supplied than quantity demanded.

Supply and Demand Analysis: An Oil Import Fee

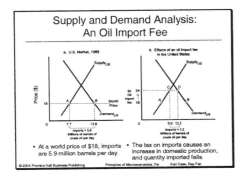

- At a world price of $18, imports are 5.9 million barrels per day.
- The tax on imports causes an increase in domestic production, and quantity imported falls.

Supply and Demand and Market Efficiency

- Supply and demand curves can be used to illustrate the idea of market efficiency, an important aspect of "normative economics."

Consumer Surplus

- **Consumer surplus** is the difference between the maximum amount a person is willing to pay for a good and its current market price.

Consumer Surplus

- Some consumers are willing to pay as much as $5 each for hamburgers.
- Since the price is only $2.50, they receive a consumer surplus of $2.50.

Consumer Surplus

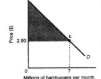

- Others are willing to pay something less than $5.00 but more than $2.50.
- Consumer surplus is the area below the demand curve and above the price level.

Producer Surplus

- *Producer surplus* is the difference between the maximum amount a producer is willing to accept to supply a good and its current market price.

Producer Surplus

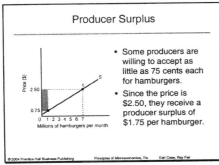

- Some producers are willing to accept as little as 75 cents each for hamburgers.
- Since the price is $2.50, they receive a producer surplus of $1.75 per hamburger.

Producer Surplus

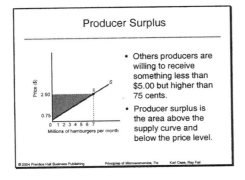

- Others producers are willing to receive something less than $5.00 but higher than 75 cents.
- Producer surplus is the area above the supply curve and below the price level.

Markets Maximize the Sum of Producer and Consumer Surplus

- Total producer and consumer surplus is highest where supply and demand curves intersect at equilibrium.
- Consumers receive benefits in excess of what they pay and producers receive compensation in excess of costs.

© 2004 Prentice Hall Business Publishing   Principles of Microeconomics, 7/e   Karl Case, Ray Fair

---

Markets Maximize the Sum of Producer and Consumer Surplus

- If the market produces too little, say 4 million instead of 7 million hamburgers per month, total producer and consumer surplus is reduced. This reduction (triangle *ABC*) is called a *deadweight loss*.

© 2004 Prentice Hall Business Publishing   Principles of Microeconomics, 7/e   Karl Case, Ray Fair

---

Potential Causes of Deadweight Loss From Under- and Overproduction

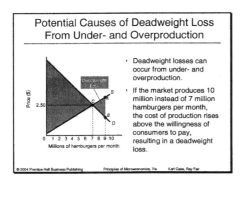

- Deadweight losses can occur from under- and overproduction.
- If the market produces 10 million instead of 7 million hamburgers per month, the cost of production rises above the willingness of consumers to pay, resulting in a deadweight loss.

© 2004 Prentice Hall Business Publishing   Principles of Microeconomics, 7/e   Karl Case, Ray Fair

Elasticity

- **Elasticity** is a general concept that can be used to quantify the response in one variable when another variable changes.

elasticity of A with respect to B = $\dfrac{\% \Delta A}{\% \Delta B}$

Price Elasticity of Demand

- A popular measure of elasticity is **price elasticity of demand** measures how responsive consumers are to changes in the price of a product.

price elasticity of demand $= \dfrac{\% \text{ change in quantity demanded}}{\% \text{ change in price}}$

- The value of demand elasticity is always negative, but it is stated in absolute terms.

Slope and Elasticity

- The value of the slope of the demand curve and the value of elasticity are not the same.
- Unlike the value of the slope, the value of elasticity is a useful measure of responsiveness.

Slope and Elasticity

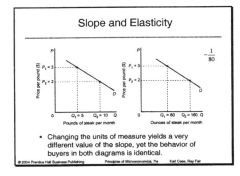

- Changing the units of measure yields a very different value of the slope, yet the behavior of buyers in both diagrams is identical.

Types of Elasticity

Hypothetical Demand Elasticities for Four Products

PRODUCT	% CHANGE IN PRICE (%ΔP)	% CHANGE IN QUANTITY DEMANDED (%ΔQ_D)		ELASTICITY (%ΔQ_D ÷ %ΔP)
Insulin	+10%	0%	0.0	Perfectly inelastic
Basic telephone service	+10%	-1%	-0.1	Inelastic
Beef	+10%	-10%	-1.0	Unitarily elastic
Bananas	+10%	-30%	-3.0	Elastic

Perfectly Elastic and Perfectly Inelastic Demand Curves

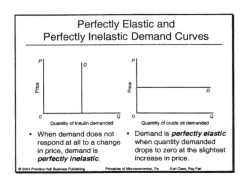

- When demand does not respond at all to a change in price, demand is **perfectly inelastic**.
- Demand is **perfectly elastic** when quantity demanded drops to zero at the slightest increase in price.

Calculating Elasticities

- Calculating percentage changes:

$$\% \text{ change in price} = \frac{P_2 - P_1}{P_1} \times 100\%$$

$$\% \text{ change in quantity demanded} = \frac{Q_2 - Q_1}{Q_1} \times 100\%$$

Calculating Elasticities

- Elasticity is a ratio of percentages.
- Computing elasticity by way of percentage changes, when price decreases from $3 to $2, yields the following result:

$$\text{price elasticity of demand} = \frac{[(10 - 5)/5] \times 100}{[(2 - 3)/3] \times 100} = \frac{100\%}{-33\%} = -3.0$$

Calculating Elasticities

- A more accurate way of computing elasticity than percentage changes is the *midpoint formula*:

$$\frac{\%\Delta Q_d}{\%\Delta P} = \frac{\frac{Q_2 - Q_1}{(Q_1 + Q_2)/2} \times 100\%}{\frac{P_2 - P_1}{(P_1 + P_2)/2} \times 100\%}$$

$$\frac{\%\Delta Q_d}{\%\Delta P} = \frac{\frac{10 - 5}{(5 + 10)/2} \times 100\%}{\frac{2 - 3}{(3 + 2)/2} \times 100\%} = \frac{\frac{5}{7.5} \times 100\%}{\frac{-1}{2.5} \times 100\%} = \frac{66.7\%}{-40.0\%} = -1.67$$

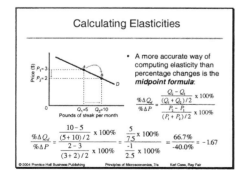

Calculating Elasticities

Here is how to interpret two different values of elasticity:

- When $\varepsilon = 0.2$, a 10% increase in price leads to a 2% decrease in quantity demanded.

- When $\varepsilon = 2.0$, a 10% increase in price leads to a 20% decrease in quantity demanded.

Elasticity Changes along a Straight-Line Demand Curve

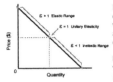

Price elasticity of demand decreases as we move downward along a straight line demand curve.

Demand is elastic in the upper range and inelastic in the lower range of the line.

Elasticity Changes along a Straight-Line Demand Curve

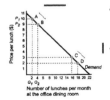

- Along the elastic range, elasticity values are greater than one.

- Along the inelastic range, elasticity values are less than one.

Elasticity and Total Revenue

$$TR = P \times Q$$

Type of demand	Value of E_d	Change in quantity versus change in price	Effect of an increase in price on total revenue	Effect of a decrease in price on total revenue
Elastic	Greater than 1.0	Larger percentage change in quantity	Total revenue decreases	Total revenue increases
Inelastic	Less than 1.0	Smaller percentage change in quantity	Total revenue increases	Total revenue decreases
Unitary elastic	Equal to 1.0	Same percentage change in quantity and price	Total revenue does not change	Total revenue does not change

- When demand is **inelastic**, price and total revenues are *directly* related. Price increases generate higher revenues.

- When demand is **elastic**, price and total revenues are *indirectly* related. Price increases generate lower revenues.

© 2004 Prentice Hall Business Publishing   Principles of Microeconomics, 7/e   Karl Case, Ray Fair

The Determinants of Demand Elasticity

- Availability of substitutes -- demand is more elastic when there are more substitutes for the product.

- Importance of the item in the budget -- demand is more elastic when the item is a more significant portion of the consumer's budget.

- Time dimension -- demand becomes more elastic over time.

© 2004 Prentice Hall Business Publishing   Principles of Microeconomics, 7/e   Karl Case, Ray Fair

Other Important Elasticities

- *Income elasticity of demand* – measures the responsiveness of demand to changes in income.

$$\text{income elasticity of demand} = \frac{\% \text{ change in quantity demanded}}{\% \text{ change in income}}$$

© 2004 Prentice Hall Business Publishing   Principles of Microeconomics, 7/e   Karl Case, Ray Fair

Other Important Elasticities

- *Cross-price elasticity of demand*: A measure of the response of the quantity of one good demanded to a change in the price of another good.

$$\text{cross-price elasticity of demand} = \frac{\%\ \text{change in quantity of } Y \text{ demanded}}{\%\ \text{change in price of } X}$$

Other Important Elasticities

- *Elasticity of supply*: A measure of the response of quantity of a good supplied to a change in price of that good. Likely to be positive in output markets.

$$\text{elasticity of supply} = \frac{\%\ \text{change in quantity supplied}}{\%\ \text{change in price}}$$

Other Important Elasticities

- *Elasticity of labor supply*: A measure of the response of labor supplied to a change in the price of labor.

$$\text{elasticity of labor supply} = \frac{\%\ \text{change in quantity of labor supplied}}{\%\ \text{change in the wage rate}}$$

Review Terms and Concepts

black market
consumer surplus
cross-price elasticity of demand
deadweight loss
elastic demand
elasticity
elasticity of labor supply
elasticity of supply
favored customers

income elasticity of demand
inelastic demand
midpoint formula
minimum wage
perfectly elastic demand
perfectly inelastic demand
price ceiling
price elasticity of demand

price floor
price rationing
producer surplus
queuing
ration coupons
unitary elasticity

© 2004 Prentice Hall Business Publishing   Principles of Microeconomics, 7/e   Karl Case, Ray Fair

---

CHAPTER 5

Household Behavior and Consumer Choice

© 2004 Prentice Hall Business Publishing   Principles of Microeconomics, 7/e   Karl Case, Ray Fair

---

Understanding the Microeconomy and the Role of Government

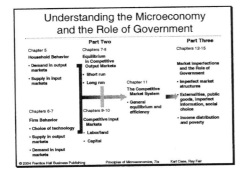

© 2004 Prentice Hall Business Publishing   Principles of Microeconomics, 7/e   Karl Case, Ray Fair

Firm and Household Decisions

- Households demand in output markets and supply labor and capital in input markets.

© 2004 Prentice Hall Business Publishing   Principles of Microeconomics, 7/e   Karl Case, Ray Fair

---

Assumptions

- A key assumption in the study of household and firm behavior is that all input and output markets are *perfectly competitive.*

© 2004 Prentice Hall Business Publishing   Principles of Microeconomics, 7/e   Karl Case, Ray Fair

---

Assumptions

- *Perfect competition* is an industry structure in which there are many firms, each small relative to the industry, producing virtually identical (or homogeneous) products and in which no firm is large enough to have any control over price.

© 2004 Prentice Hall Business Publishing   Principles of Microeconomics, 7/e   Karl Case, Ray Fair

Assumptions

- We also assume that households and firms possess all the information they need to make market choices.

  - *Perfect knowledge* is the assumption that households posses a knowledge of the qualities and prices of everything available in the market, and that firms have all available information concerning wage rates, capital costs, and output prices.

Household Choice in Output Markets

- Every household must make *three basic decisions:*

  1. How much of each product, or output, to demand.
  2. How much labor to supply.
  3. How much to spend today and how much to save for the future.

The Determinants of Household Demand
(as seen in Chapter 3)

Factors that influence the quantity of a given good or service demanded by a single household include:

- The *price of the product* in question.
- The *income* available to the household.
- The household's amount of *accumulated wealth*.
- The *prices of related products* available to the household.
- The household's *tastes and preferences*.
- The household's *expectations* about future income, wealth, and prices.

The Budget Constraint

- The *budget constraint* refers to the limits imposed on household choices by income, wealth, and product prices.
- A *choice set* or *opportunity set* is the set of options that is defined by a budget constraint.

The Budget Constraint

- A *budget constraint* separates those combinations of goods and services that are available, given limited income, from those that are not.
- The available combinations make up the *opportunity set*.

The Budget Constraint

Possible Budget Choices of a Person Earning $1,000 Per Month After Taxes

OPTION	RENT	FOOD	OTHER	TOTAL	AVAILABLE?
A	$ 400	$250	$350	$1,000	Yes
B	600	200	200	1,000	Yes
C	700	150	150	1,000	Yes
D	1,000	100	100	1,200	No

- The real cost of a good or service is its *opportunity cost*, and opportunity cost is determined by relative prices.

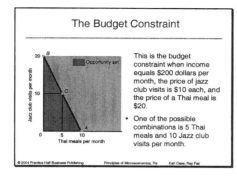

The Budget Constraint

This is the budget constraint when income equals $200 dollars per month, the price of jazz club visits is $10 each, and the price of a Thai meal is $20.

- One of the possible combinations is 5 Thai meals and 10 Jazz club visits per month.

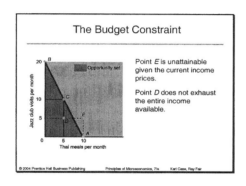

The Budget Constraint

Point *E* is unattainable given the current income prices.

Point *D* does not exhaust the entire income available.

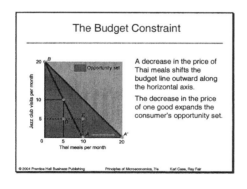

The Budget Constraint

A decrease in the price of Thai meals shifts the budget line outward along the horizontal axis.

The decrease in the price of one good expands the consumer's opportunity set.

The Basis of Choice: Utility

- **Utility** is the satisfaction, or reward, a product yields relative to its alternatives. The basis of choice.
- **Marginal utility** is the additional satisfaction gained by the consumption or use of one more unit of something.

© 2004 Prentice Hall Business Publishing   Principles of Microeconomics, 7/e   Karl Case, Ray Fair

---

Diminishing Marginal Utility

- The **law of diminishing marginal utility:**

  The more of one good consumed in a given period, the less satisfaction (utility) generated by consuming each additional (marginal) unit of the same good.

© 2004 Prentice Hall Business Publishing   Principles of Microeconomics, 7/e   Karl Case, Ray Fair

---

Diminishing Marginal Utility

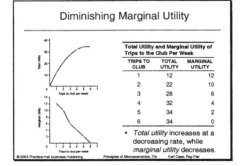

Total Utility and Marginal Utility of Trips to the Club Per Week

TRIPS TO CLUB	TOTAL UTILITY	MARGINAL UTILITY
1	12	12
2	22	10
3	28	6
4	32	4
5	34	2
6	34	0

- *Total utility* increases at a decreasing rate, while *marginal utility* decreases.

© 2004 Prentice Hall Business Publishing   Principles of Microeconomics, 7/e   Karl Case, Ray Fair

Diminishing Marginal Utility and Downward-Sloping Demand

- Diminishing marginal utility helps to explain why demand slopes down.
- Marginal utility falls with each additional unit consumed, so people are not willing to pay as much.

© 2004 Prentice Hall Business Publishing   Principles of Microeconomics, 7/e   Karl Case, Ray Fair

Income and Substitution Effects

Price changes affect households in two ways:

- **The *income effect*:** Consumption changes because purchasing power changes.
- The ***substitution effect*:** Consumption changes because opportunity costs change.

© 2004 Prentice Hall Business Publishing   Principles of Microeconomics, 7/e   Karl Case, Ray Fair

Income and Substitution Effects of a Price Change (for normal goods)

Income effect:

- When the price of a product falls, a consumer has more purchasing power with the same amount of income.
- When the price of a product rises, a consumer has less purchasing power with the same amount of income.

Substitution effect:

- When the price of a product falls, that product becomes more attractive relative to potential substitutes.
- When the price of a product rises, that product becomes less attractive relative to potential substitutes.

© 2004 Prentice Hall Business Publishing   Principles of Microeconomics, 7/e   Karl Case, Ray Fair

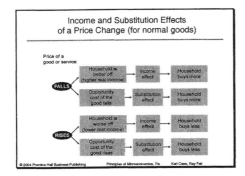

Income and Substitution Effects
of a Price Change (for normal goods)

Consumer Surplus

- *Consumer surplus* is the difference between the maximum amount a person is willing to pay for a good and its current market price.

- Consumer surplus measurement is a key element in *cost-benefit analysis*—the formal technique by which the benefits of a public project are weighed against its costs.

The Diamond/Water Paradox

- Water is plentiful.
- If the price of water was zero, you might argue that water has no value. But it does. Consumers enjoy a huge consumer surplus from water consumption.
- Household willingness to pay far exceeds the zero price.

The Diamond/Water Paradox

The lesson of the
diamond/water paradox is
that:

1. the things with the greatest
value in use frequently have
little or no value in exchange,
and

2. the things with the greatest
value in exchange frequently
have little or no value in use.

Household Choice in Input Markets

As in output markets, households face
constrained choices in input markets.
They must decide:

1. Whether to work
2. How much to work
3. What kind of a job to work at

These decisions are affected by:

1. The availability of jobs
2. Market wage rates
3. The skill possessed by the
household

The Price of Leisure

- The wage rate can be thought of as the
price—or the opportunity cost— of the
benefits of either unpaid work or leisure.

Average hourly earnings of production or non-
supervisory workers on non-farm payrolls in February
of 2003

	Hourly wage rate
Average—all workers	$15.08
Construction workers	18.20
Manufacturing	15.58
Excluding overtime	14.84
Retail Trade	10.22
Finance, Insurance and Real Estate	16.76

The Trade-Off Facing Households

- The decision to enter the workforce involves a trade-off between wages on the one hand, and leisure and the value of nonmarket production on the other.

The Labor Supply Curve

- The **labor supply curve** is a diagram that shows the quantity of labor supplied at different wage rates.

Income and Substitution Effects of a Wage Change

- An increase in the wage rate affects households in two ways, known as the ... me effects.

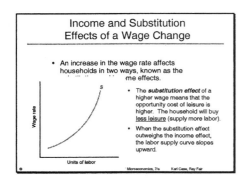

- The **substitution effect** of a higher wage means that the opportunity cost of leisure is higher. The household will buy less leisure (supply more labor).
- When the substitution effect outweighs the income effect, the labor supply curve slopes upward.

Income and Substitution Effects of a Wage Change

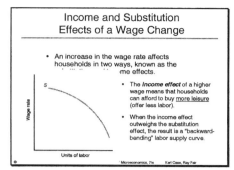

- An increase in the wage rate affects households in two ways, known as the ... ...me effects.

  - The *income effect* of a higher wage means that households can afford to buy more leisure (offer less labor).

  - When the income effect outweighs the substitution effect, the result is a "backward-bending" labor supply curve.

Microeconomics, 7/e   Karl Case, Ray Fair

Saving and Borrowing: Present Versus Future Consumption

- Households can use present income to finance future spending (i.e., save), or they can use future funds to finance present spending (i.e., borrow).

- The *financial capital market* is the complex set of institutions in which suppliers of capital (households that save) and the demand for capital (business firms that invest) interact.

© 2004 Prentice Hall Business Publishing   Principles of Microeconomics, 7/e   Karl Case, Ray Fair

Saving and Borrowing: Present Versus Future Consumption

- In deciding how much to save and how much to spend today, interest rates define the opportunity cost of present consumption in terms of foregone future consumption.

Sample interest rates early in 2003

	Interest Rate
National average on bank money market accounts	0.74%
Two-year treasury notes	1.75%
Ten-year treasury bonds	4.10%
National average on new car loans	7.77%
30-year fixed rate mortgage	5.92%

© 2004 Prentice Hall Business Publishing   Principles of Microeconomics, 7/e   Karl Case, Ray Fair

Saving and Borrowing: Present Versus Future Consumption

An increase in the interest rate also has substitution and income effects, as follows:

- *Income effect*: Households will now earn more on all previous savings, so they will save <u>less</u>.

- *Substitution effect*: The opportunity cost of present consumption is now higher; given the law of demand, the household will save <u>more</u>.

Review Terms and Concepts

budget constraint

change set or opportunity set

consumer surplus

cost-benefit analysis

diamond/water paradox

financial capital market

homogeneous products

income effect of a price change

labor supply curve

law of diminishing marginal utility

marginal utility

perfect competition

perfect knowledge

substitution effect of a price change

total utility

utility

utility-maximizing rule

Appendix: Indifference Curves

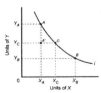

- An *indifference curve* is a set of points , each point representing a combination of goods *X* and *Y*, all of which yields the same total utility.

- The consumer is worse of at *A'* than at *A*.

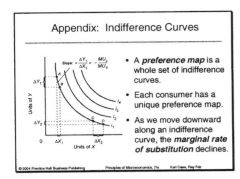

Appendix: Indifference Curves

- A *preference map* is a whole set of indifference curves.
- Each consumer has a unique preference map.
- As we move downward along an indifference curve, the *marginal rate of substitution* declines.

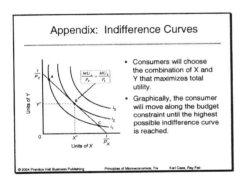

Appendix: Indifference Curves

- Consumers will choose the combination of X and Y that maximizes total utility.
- Graphically, the consumer will move along the budget constraint until the highest possible indifference curve is reached.

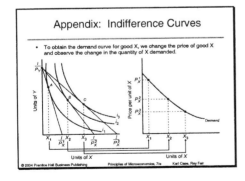

Appendix: Indifference Curves

- To obtain the demand curve for good X, we change the price of good X and observe the change in the quantity of X demanded.

CHAPTER 6

The Production Process:
The Behavior of
Profit-Maximizing Firms

© 2004 Prentice Hall Business Publishing   Principles of Microeconomics, 7/e   Karl Case, Ray Fair

---

Production

Central to our analysis is
production, the process by
which inputs are combined,
transformed, and turned
into outputs.

© 2004 Prentice Hall Business Publishing   Principles of Microeconomics, 7/e   Karl Case, Ray Fair

---

Firm and Household Decisions

• Firms *demand*
factors of
production in
input markets
and *supply* goods
and services in
output markets.

© 2004 Prentice Hall Business Publishing   Principles of Microeconomics, 7/e   Karl Case, Ray Fair

What Is A *Firm*?

- A *firm* is an organization that comes into being when a person or a group of people decides to produce a good or service to meet a perceived demand. Most firms exist to make a profit.

- Production is not limited to firms.

- Many important differences exist between firms.

Perfect Competition

Perfect competition is an industry structure in which there are:

- *many firms*, each small relative to the industry,

- producing virtually *identical products* and

- in which *no* firm is large enough to have any *control over prices*.

- In perfectly competitive industries, new competitors can *freely enter and exit* the market.

Homogeneous Products

- *Homogeneous products* are undifferentiated products; products that are identical to, or indistinguishable from, one another.

- In a perfectly competitive market, individual firms are *price-takers*. Firms have no control over price; price is determined by the interaction of market supply and demand.

Demand Facing a Single Firm in a Perfectly Competitive Market

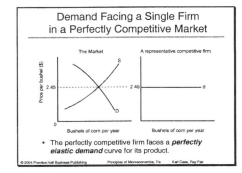

- The perfectly competitive firm faces a **perfectly elastic demand** curve for its product.

© 2004 Prentice Hall Business Publishing   Principles of Microeconomics, 7/e   Karl Case, Ray Fair

The Behavior of Profit-Maximizing Firms

- The three decisions that all firms must make include:

1.
How much output to supply

2.
Which production technology to use

3.
How much of each input to demand

© 2004 Prentice Hall Business Publishing   Principles of Microeconomics, 7/e   Karl Case, Ray Fair

Profits and Economic Costs

- **Profit (economic profit)** is the difference between total revenue and total economic cost.

economic profit = total revenue − total economic cost

- **Total revenue** is the amount received from the sale of the product:

$$(q \ x \ P)$$

© 2004 Prentice Hall Business Publishing   Principles of Microeconomics, 7/e   Karl Case, Ray Fair

Profits and Economic Costs

- *Total cost (total economic cost)* is the total of
  1. Out of pocket costs,
  2. Normal rate of return on capital, and
  3. Opportunity cost of each factor of production.

Profits and Economic Costs

- The *rate of return,* often referred to as the yield of the investment, is the annual flow of net income generated by an investment expressed as a percentage of the total investment.

Profits and Economic Costs

- The *normal rate of return* is a rate of return on capital that is just sufficient to keep owners and investors satisfied.
  - For relatively risk-free firms, the normal rate of return be nearly the same as the interest rate on risk-free government bonds.

Profits and Economic Costs

- *Out-of-pocket costs* are sometimes referred to as *explicit costs* or *accounting costs*.

- *Economic costs*, often referred to as *implicit cots*, include the full opportunity cost of every input.

Calculating Total Revenue, Total Cost, and Profit

Initial Investment:	$20,000
Market Interest Rate Available:	.10 or 10%
Total Revenue (3,000 belts x $10 each)	$30,000
Costs	
Belts from supplier	$15,000
Labor Cost	14,000
Normal return/opportunity cost of capital ($20,000 x .10)	2,000
Total Cost	$31,000
Profit = total revenue – total cost	– $ 1,000*
*There is a loss of $1,000.	

Short-Run Versus Long-Run Decisions

- The *short run* is a period of time for which two conditions hold:

  1. The firm is operating under a fixed scale (or fixed factor) of production, and

  2. Firms can neither enter nor exit the industry.

Short-Run Versus Long-Run Decisions

- The *long run* is a period of time for which there are no fixed factors of production. Firms can increase or decrease scale of operation, and new firms can enter and existing firms can exit the industry.

The Bases of Decisions

- The fundamental things to know with the objective of maximizing profit are:

1.
The market price of the output

2.
The techniques of production that are available

3.
The prices of inputs

Determining the Optimal Method of Production

Price of output   Production techniques   Input prices

|
Determines total revenue

Determine total cost and optimal method of production

Total revenue
– Total cost with optimal method
=Total profit

- The *optimal method of production* is the method that minimizes cost.

The Production Process

- *Production technology* refers to the quantitative relationship between inputs and outputs.

- A *labor-intensive technology* relies heavily on human labor instead of capital.

- A *capital-intensive technology* relies heavily on capital instead of human labor.

The Production Function

- The *production function* or *total product function* is a numerical or mathematical expression of a relationship between inputs and outputs. It shows units of total product as a function of units of inputs.

Marginal Product

- *Marginal product* is the additional output that can be produced by adding one more unit of a specific input, *ceteris paribus*.

$$\text{marginal product of labor} = \frac{\text{change in total product}}{\text{change in units of labor used}}$$

The Law of Diminishing Marginal Returns

- The *law of diminishing marginal returns* states that:

  When additional units of a variable input are added to fixed inputs, the marginal product of the variable input declines.

Average Product

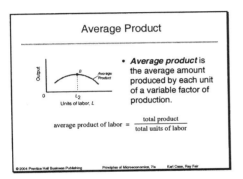

- *Average product* is the average amount produced by each unit of a variable factor of production.

$$\text{average product of labor} = \frac{\text{total product}}{\text{total units of labor}}$$

Production Function for Sandwiches

Production Function

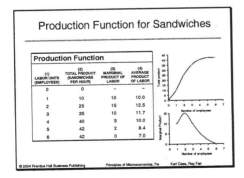

(1) LABOR UNITS (EMPLOYEES)	(2) TOTAL PRODUCT (SANDWICHES PER HOUR)	(3) MARGINAL PRODUCT OF LABOR	(4) AVERAGE PRODUCT OF LABOR
0	0	--	--
1	10	10	10.0
2	25	15	12.5
3	35	10	11.7
4	40	5	10.0
5	42	2	8.4
6	42	0	7.0

Total, Average, and Marginal Product

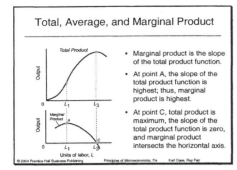

- Marginal product is the slope of the total product function.
- At point A, the slope of the total product function is highest; thus, marginal product is highest.
- At point C, total product is maximum, the slope of the total product function is zero, and marginal product intersects the horizontal axis.

Total, Average, and Marginal Product

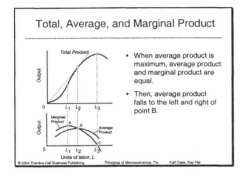

- When average product is maximum, average product and marginal product are equal.
- Then, average product falls to the left and right of point B.

Total, Average, and Marginal Product

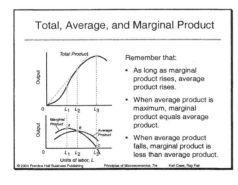

Remember that:

- As long as marginal product rises, average product rises.
- When average product is maximum, marginal product equals average product.
- When average product falls, marginal product is less than average product.

Production Functions with Two Variable Factors of Production

- In many production processes, inputs work together and are viewed as complementary.
  - For example, increases in capital usage lead to increases in the productivity of labor.

Inputs Required to Produce 100 Diapers Using Alternative Technologies		
TECHNOLOGY	UNITS OF CAPITAL (K)	UNITS OF LABOR (L)
A	2	10
B	3	6
C	4	4
D	6	3
E	10	2

- Given the technologies available, the cost-minimizing choice depends on input prices.

Production Functions with Two Variable Factors of Production

Cost-Minimizing Choice Among Alternative Technologies (100 Diapers)

(1) TECHNOLOGY	(2) UNITS OF CAPITAL (K)	(3) UNITS OF LABOR (L)	(4) COST WHEN $P_L = \$1\ P_K = \$1$	(5) COST WHEN $P_L = \$5\ P_K = \$1$
A	2	10	$12	$52
B	3	6	9	33
C	4	4	8	24
D	6	3	9	21
E	10	2	12	20

Review Terms and Concepts

Accounting costs	Marginal product
Average product	Normal rate of return
Capital-intensive technology	Optimal method of production
Economic costs	Out-of-pocket costs
Economic profit	Perfect competition
Fixed costs	production
Firm	Production function or total product function
Homogeneous products	Production technology
Implicit costs	Profit (economic profit)
Labor-intensive technology	Short run
Law of diminishing returns	Total cost (total economic cost)
Long run	Total revenue

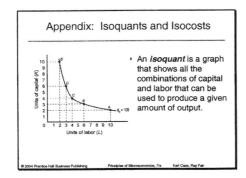

An *isoquant* is a graph that shows all the combinations of capital and labor that can be used to produce a given amount of output.

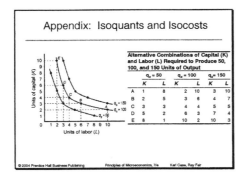

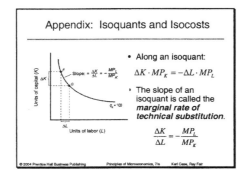

- Along an isoquant:

$$\Delta K \cdot MP_K = -\Delta L \cdot MP_L$$

- The slope of an isoquant is called the *marginal rate of technical substitution*.

$$\frac{\Delta K}{\Delta L} = -\frac{MP_L}{MP_K}$$

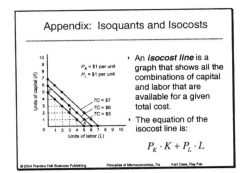

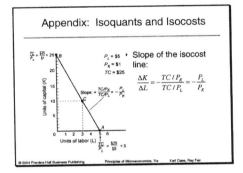

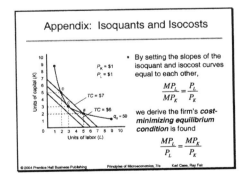

Appendix: Isoquants and Isocosts

- Plotting a series of cost-minimizing combinations of inputs (at points A, B, and C), yields a *cost curve*.

© 2004 Prentice Hall Business Publishing   Principles of Microeconomics, 7/e   Karl Case, Ray Fair

---

CHAPTER 7

Short-Run Costs and Output Decisions

Prepared by: Fernando Quijano
and Yvonn Quijano

© 2004 Prentice Hall Business Publishing   Principles of Microeconomics, 7/e   Karl Case, Ray Fair

---

Decisions Facing Firms

DECISIONS	are based on	INFORMATION
1. How much output to supply	2. Which production technology to use	1. The market price of the output
3. How much of each input to demand		2. The techniques of production that are available
		3. The prices of inputs

© 2004 Prentice Hall Business Publishing   Principles of Microeconomics, 7/e   Karl Case, Ray Fair

Costs in the Short Run

- The *short run* is a period of time for which two conditions hold:

  1. The firm is operating under a fixed scale (fixed factor) of production, and

  2. Firms can neither enter nor exit an industry.

Costs in the Short Run

- *Fixed cost* is any cost that does not depend on the firm's level of output. These costs are incurred even if the firm is producing nothing. There are no fixed costs in the long run.

- *Variable cost* is a cost that depends on the level of production chosen.

$$TC = TFC + TVC$$

Total Cost = Total Fixed + Total Variable
Cost   Cost

Total Fixed Cost (*TFC*)

- *Total fixed costs (TFC)* or *overhead* refers to the total of all costs that do not change with output, even if output is zero.

- Another name for fixed costs in the short run is *sunk costs* is because firms have no choice but to pay for them.

Average Fixed Cost (*AFC*)

- **Average fixed cost (AFC)** is the total fixed cost (*TFC*) divided by the number of units of output (*q*):

$$AFC = \frac{TFC}{q}$$

- **Spreading overhead** is the process of dividing total fixed costs by more units of output. Average fixed cost declines as quantity rises.

Short-Run Fixed Cost
(Total and Average) of a Hypothetical Firm

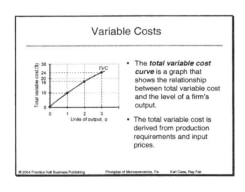

(1) q	(2) TFC	(3) AFC (TFC/q)
0	$1,000	$ —
1	1,000	1,000
2	1,000	500
3	1,000	333
4	1,000	250
5	1,000	200

- As output increases, total fixed cost remains constant and average fixed cost declines.

Variable Costs

- The **total variable cost curve** is a graph that shows the relationship between total variable cost and the level of a firm's output.

- The total variable cost is derived from production requirements and input prices.

Derivation of Total Variable Cost Schedule from Technology and Factor Prices

PRODUCT	USING TECHNIQUE	UNITS OF INPUT REQUIRED (PRODUCTION FUNCTION)		TOTAL VARIABLE COST ASSUMING $P_K = \$2, P_L = \$1$ $TVC = (K \times P_K) + (L \times P_L)$
		K	L	
1 Units of	A	4	4	$(4 \times \$2) + (4 \times \$1) = \$12$
output	B	2	6	$(2 \times \$2) + (6 \times \$1) = \$10$
2 Units of	A	7	6	$(7 \times \$2) + (6 \times \$1) = \$20$
output	B	4	10	$(4 \times \$2) + (10 \times \$1) = \$18$
3 Units of	A	9	6	$(9 \times \$2) + (6 \times \$1) = \$24$
output	B	6	14	$(6 \times \$2) + (14 \times \$1) = \$26$

- The total variable cost curve shows the cost of production using the best available technique at each output level, given current factor prices.

Marginal Cost (*MC*)

- **Marginal cost (MC)** is the increase in total cost that results from producing one more unit of output. Marginal cost reflects changes in variable costs.

UNITS OF OUTPUT	TOTAL VARIABLE COSTS ($)	MARGINAL COSTS ($)
0	0	0
1	10	10
2	18	8
3	24	6

The Shape of the Marginal Cost Curve in the Short Run

- In the short run every firm is constrained by some fixed input that:
  1. leads to diminishing returns to variable inputs, and
  2. limits its capacity to produce.

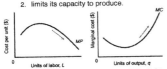

Graphing Total Variable Costs and Marginal Costs

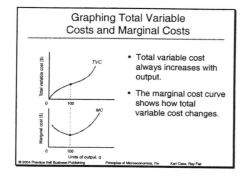

- Total variable cost always increases with output.
- The marginal cost curve shows how total variable cost changes.

© 2004 Prentice Hall Business Publishing   Principles of Microeconomics, 7/e   Karl Case, Ray Fair

---

Average Variable Cost (*AVC*)

- **Average variable cost (AVC)** is the total variable cost divided by the number of units of output.

$$AVC = \frac{TVC}{q}$$

- Marginal cost is the cost of *one additional unit*, while average variable cost is the *variable cost per unit* of *all* the units being produced.

© 2004 Prentice Hall Business Publishing   Principles of Microeconomics, 7/e   Karl Case, Ray Fair

---

Short-Run Costs of a Hypothetical Firm

(1) q	(2) TVC	(3) MC (Δ TVC)	(4) AVC (TVC/q)	(5) TFC	(6) TC (TVC + TFC)	(7) AFC (TFC/q)	(8) ATC (TC/q or AFC + AVC)
0	$ 0	$ -	$ -	$1,000	$ 1,000	$ -	$ -
1	10	10	10	1,000	1,010	1,000	1,010
2	18	8	9	1,000	1,018	500	509
3	24	6	8	1,000	1,024	333	341
4	32	8	8	1,000	1,032	250	258
5	42	10	8.4	1,000	1,042	200	208.4
-	-	-	-	-	-	-	-
-	-	-	-	-	-	-	-
-	-	-	-	-	-	-	-
500	8,000	20	16	1,000	9,000	2	18

© 2004 Prentice Hall Business Publishing   Principles of Microeconomics, 7/e   Karl Case, Ray Fair

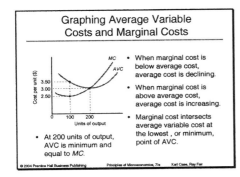

Graphing Average Variable Costs and Marginal Costs

- When marginal cost is below average cost, average cost is declining.
- When marginal cost is above average cost, average cost is increasing.
- Marginal cost intersects average variable cost at the lowest, or minimum, point of AVC.
- At 200 units of output, AVC is minimum and equal to *MC*.

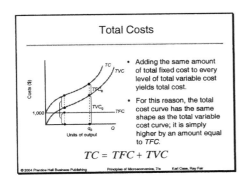

Total Costs

- Adding the same amount of total fixed cost to every level of total variable cost yields total cost.
- For this reason, the total cost curve has the same shape as the total variable cost curve; it is simply higher by an amount equal to *TFC*.

$$TC = TFC + TVC$$

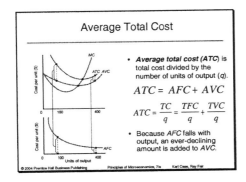

Average Total Cost

- **Average total cost (ATC)** is total cost divided by the number of units of output (*q*).

$$ATC = AFC + AVC$$

$$ATC = \frac{TC}{q} = \frac{TFC}{q} + \frac{TVC}{q}$$

- Because *AFC* falls with output, an ever-declining amount is added to *AVC*.

The Relationship Between Average Total Cost and Marginal Cost

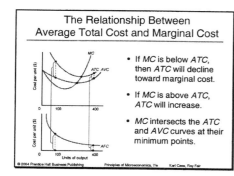

- If *MC* is below *ATC*, then *ATC* will decline toward marginal cost.

- If *MC* is above *ATC*, *ATC* will increase.

- *MC* intersects the *ATC* and *AVC* curves at their minimum points.

Output Decisions: Revenues, Costs, and Profit Maximization

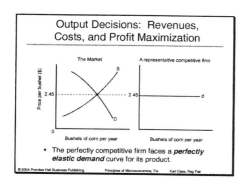

- The perfectly competitive firm faces a **perfectly elastic demand** curve for its product.

Total Revenue (*TR*) and Marginal Revenue (*MR*)

- **Total revenue (TR)** is the total amount that a firm takes in from the sale of its output.

$$TR = P \times q$$

- **Marginal revenue (MR)** is the additional revenue that a firm takes in when it increases output by one additional unit.

- In perfect competition, $P = MR$.

Comparing Costs and Revenues to Maximize Profit

- The profit-maximizing level of output for all firms is the output level where $MR = MC$.

- In perfect competition, $MR = P$, therefore, the firm will produce up to the point where the price of its output is just equal to short-run marginal cost.

- *The key idea here is that firms will produce as long as marginal revenue exceeds marginal cost.*

Comparing Costs and Revenues to Maximize Profit

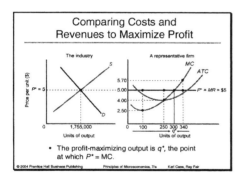

- The profit-maximizing output is q^*, the point at which $P^* = MC$.

Profit Analysis for a Simple Firm

(1) q	(2) TFC	(3) TVC	(4) MC	(5) P = MR	(6) TR (P x q)	(7) TC (TFC + TVC)	(8) PROFIT (TR – TC)
0	$ 10	$ 0	$ –	$ 15	$ 0	$ 10	$ -10
1	10	10	10	15	15	20	-5
2	10	15	5	15	30	25	5
3	10	20	5	15	45	30	15
4	10	30	10	15	60	40	20
5	10	50	20	15	75	60	15
6	10	80	30	15	90	90	0

The Short-Run Supply Curve

- At any market price, the marginal cost curve shows the output level that maximizes profit. Thus, the marginal cost curve of a perfectly competitive profit-maximizing firm is the firm's short-run supply curve.

Review Terms and Concepts

average fixed cost (AFC)	sunk costs
average total cost (ATC)	total cost (TC)
average variable cost (AVC)	total fixed cost (TFC)
fixed cost	total revenue (TR)
marginal cost (MC)	total variable cost (TVC)
marginal revenue (MR)	total variable cost curve
spreading overhead	variable cost

CHAPTER 8

Long-Run Costs and Output Decisions

Prepared by: Fernando Quijano and Yvonn Quijano

Short-Run Conditions and Long-Run Directions

- *Profit* is the difference between total revenue and total economic cost.

- Total economic cost includes a *normal rate of return,* or the rate that is just sufficient to keep current investors interested in the industry.

- **Breaking even** is a situation in which a firm earns exactly a normal rate of return.

Maximizing Profits

Blue Velvet Car Wash Weekly Costs

TOTAL FIXED COSTS (TFC)		TOTAL VARIABLE COSTS (TVC) (800 WASHES)		TOTAL COSTS (TC = TFC + TVC)	$ 3,600
1. Normal return to investors	$ 1,000	1. Labor	$1,000	Total revenue (TR) at P = $5 (800 x $5)	$ 4,000
2. Other fixed costs (maintenance contract, insurance, etc.)	1,000	2. Materials	600	Profit (TR – TC)	$ 400
	$ 2,000		$1,600		

- Revenue is sufficient to cover both fixed costs of $2,000 and variable costs of $1,600, leaving a positive economic profit of $400 per week.

Firm Earning Positive Profits in the Short Run

- To maximize profit, the firm sets the level of output where marginal revenue equals marginal cost.

Firm Earning Positive Profits in the Short Run

- Profit is the difference between total revenue and total cost.

Minimizing Losses

- **Operating profit (or loss)** or **net operating revenue** equals total revenue minus total variable cost (TR – TVC).
  - If revenues exceed variable costs, operating profit is positive and can be used to offset fixed costs and reduce losses, and it will pay the firm to keep operating.

Minimizing Losses

- **Operating profit (or loss)** or **net operating revenue** equals total revenue minus total variable cost (TR – TVC).
  - If revenues are smaller than variable costs, the firm suffers operating losses that push total losses above fixed costs. In this case, the firm can minimize its losses by shutting down.

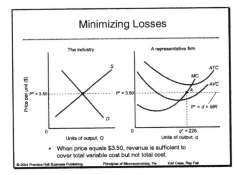

Minimizing Losses

The industry / **A representative firm**

- When price equals $3.50, revenue is sufficient to cover total variable cost but not total cost.

© 2004 Prentice Hall Business Publishing   Principles of Microeconomics, 7/e   Karl Case, Ray Fair

---

Minimizing Losses

A Firm Will Operate If Total Revenue Covers Total Variable Cost

CASE 1: SHUT DOWN		CASE 2: OPERATE AT PRICE = $3	
Total Revenue ($q = 0$)	$ 0	Total Revenue ($3 x 800)	$ 2,400
Fixed costs	$ 2,000	Fixed costs	$ 2,000
Variable costs	+ 0	Variable costs	+ 1,800
Total costs	$ 2,000	Total costs	$ 3,800
Profit/loss ($TR - TC$)	– $ 2,000	Operating profit/loss ($TR - TVC$)	$ 800
		Total profit/loss ($TR - TC$)	–$ 1,200

© 2004 Prentice Hall Business Publishing   Principles of Microeconomics, 7/e   Karl Case, Ray Fair

---

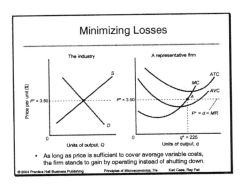

Minimizing Losses

The industry / **A representative firm**

- As long as price is sufficient to cover average variable costs, the firm stands to gain by operating instead of shutting down.

© 2004 Prentice Hall Business Publishing   Principles of Microeconomics, 7/e   Karl Case, Ray Fair

Minimizing Losses

The industry

A representative firm

Losses   Operating profit
Total fixed costs

- The difference between *ATC* and *AVC* equals *AFC*.
  Then, *AFC* × *q* = *TFC*.

© 2004 Prentice Hall Business Publishing   Principles of Microeconomics, 7/e   Karl Case, Ray Fair

Shutting Down to Minimize Loss

A Firm Will Shut Down If Total Revenue Is Less Than Total Variable Cost

CASE 1: SHUT DOWN		CASE 2: OPERATE AT PRICE = $1.50	
Total Revenue (*q* = 0)	$ 0	Total revenue ($1.50 x 800)	$ 1,200
Fixed costs	$ 2,000	Fixed costs	$ 2,000
Variable costs	+ 0	Variable costs	+ 1,600
Total costs	$ 2,000	Total costs	$ 3,600
Profit/loss (*TR* − *TC*)	− $ 2,000	Operating profit/loss (*TR* − *TVC*)	− $ 400
		Total profit/loss (*TR* − *TC*)	− $ 2,400

© 2004 Prentice Hall Business Publishing   Principles of Microeconomics, 7/e   Karl Case, Ray Fair

Short-Run Supply Curve
of a Perfectly Competitive Firm

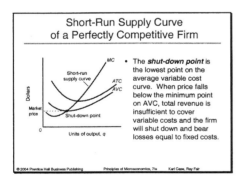

- The **shut-down point** is the lowest point on the average variable cost curve. When price falls below the minimum point on AVC, total revenue is insufficient to cover variable costs and the firm will shut down and bear losses equal to fixed costs.

© 2004 Prentice Hall Business Publishing   Principles of Microeconomics, 7/e   Karl Case, Ray Fair

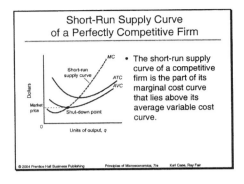

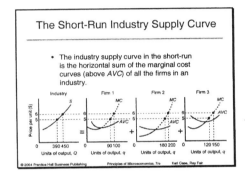

Profits, Losses, and Perfectly Competitive
Firm Decisions in the Long and Short Run

	SHORT-RUN CONDITION	SHORT-RUN DECISION	LONG-RUN DECISION
Profits	TR > TC	P = MC: operate	Expand: new firms enter
Losses	1. With operating profit	P = MC: operate	Contract: firms exit
	(TR ≥ TVC)	(losses < fixed costs)	
	2. With operating losses	Shut down:	Contract: firms exit
	(TR < TVC)	losses = fixed costs	

- In the short-run, firms have to decide how much to produce in the current scale of plant.
- In the long-run, firms have to choose among many potential scales of plant.

© 2004 Prentice Hall Business Publishing   Principles of Microeconomics, 7/e   Karl Case, Ray Fair

Long-Run Costs: Economies and Diseconomies of Scale

- *Increasing returns to scale*, or *economies of scale,* refers to an increase in a firm's scale of production, which leads to *lower* average costs per unit produced.

Weekly Costs Showing Economies of Scale in Egg Production

JONES FARM	TOTAL WEEKLY COSTS
15 hours of labor (implicit value $8 per hour)	$120
Feed, other variable costs	25
Transport costs	15
Land and capital costs attributable to egg production	17
	$177
Total output	2,400 eggs
Average cost	$.074 per egg

CHICKEN LITTLE EGG FARMS INC.	TOTAL WEEKLY COSTS
Labor	$ 5,128
Feed, other variable costs	4,115
Transport costs	2,431
Land and capital costs	19,230
	$30,904
Total output	1,800,000 eggs
Average cost	$.019 per egg

A Firm Exhibiting Economies of Scale

- The long run average cost curve of a firm exhibiting economies of scale is downward-sloping.

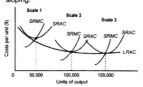

The Long-Run Average Cost Curve

- The *long-run average cost curve (LRAC)* is a graph that shows the different scales on which a firm can choose to operate in the long-run. Each scale of operation defines a different short-run.

Constant Returns to Scale

- *Constant returns to scale* refers to an increase in a firm's scale of production, which has *no effect* on average costs per unit produced.

Decreasing Returns to Scale

- *Decreasing returns to scale*, or *diseconomies of scale*, refers to an increase in a firm's scale of production, which leads to *higher* average costs per unit produced.

A Firm Exhibiting Economies and Diseconomies of Scale

- The *LRAC* curve of a firm that eventually exhibits diseconomies of scale becomes upward-sloping.

Optimal Scale of Plant

- The *optimal scale of plant* is the scale that minimizes average cost.

Long-Run Adjustments to Short-Run Conditions

- Firms expand in the long-run when increasing returns to scale are available.

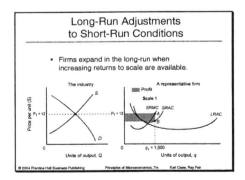

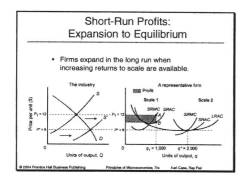

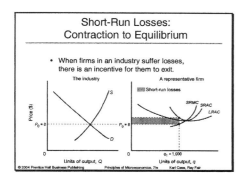

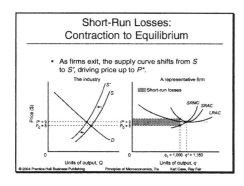

Short-Run Losses:
Contraction to Equilibrium

- The industry eventually returns to long-run equilibrium and losses are eliminated.

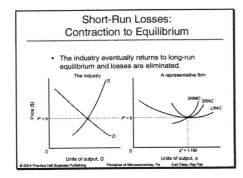

© 2004 Prentice Hall Business Publishing   Principles of Microeconomics, 7/e   Karl Case, Ray Fair

---

Long-Run Competitive Equilibrium

- In the long run, equilibrium price (P^*) is equal to long-run average cost, short-run marginal cost, and short-run average cost. Profits are driven to zero.

$$P^* = SRMC = SRAC = LRAC$$

© 2004 Prentice Hall Business Publishing   Principles of Microeconomics, 7/e   Karl Case, Ray Fair

---

The Long-Run Adjustment Mechanism:
Investment Flows Toward Profit Opportunities

- The central idea in our discussion of entry, exit, expansion, and contraction is this:
  - In efficient markets, investment capital flows toward profit opportunities.
  - The actual process is complex and varies from industry to industry.

© 2004 Prentice Hall Business Publishing   Principles of Microeconomics, 7/e   Karl Case, Ray Fair

Long-Run Adjustment Mechanism: Investment Flows Toward Profit Opportunities

- The central idea in our discussion of entry, exit, expansion, and contraction is this:

  - Investment—in the form of new firms and expanding old firms—will over time tend to favor those industries in which profits are being made, and over time industries in which firms are suffering losses will gradually contract from disinvestment.

Review Terms and Concepts

breakeven point

constant return to scale

decreasing returns to scale, or diseconomies of scale

increasing returns to scale, or economies of scale

long-run average cost curve (LRAC)

long-run competitive equilibrium

operating profit (or loss) or net operating revenue

optimal scale of plant

short-run industry supply curve

shut-down point

long-run competitive equilibrium: P = SRMC = SRAC = LRAC

Appendix: External Economies and Diseconomies and the Long-Run Industry Supply Curve

- Economies of scale that are found within the individual firm are called *internal economies of scale.*

- *External economies of scale* describe economies or diseconomies of scale on an industry-wide basis.

Appendix: External Economies and Diseconomies and the Long-Run Industry Supply Curve

- The *long-run industry supply curve (LRIS)* traces output over time as the industry expands.

- When an industry enjoys external economies, its long-run supply curve slopes down. Such an industry is called a *decreasing-cost industry.*

Appendix: External Economies and Diseconomies and the Long-Run Industry Supply Curve

Construction Activity and the Price of Lumber Products, 1991 - 1994

YEAR	MONTHLY AVERAGE, NEW HOUSING PERMITS	PERCENTAGE INCREASE OVER THE PREVIOUS YEAR	PERCENTAGE CHANGE IN THE PRICE OF LUMBER PRODUCTS	PERCENTAGE CHANGE IN CONSUMER PRICES
1991	79,500	-	-	-
1992	92,167	+ 15.9	+ 14.7	+ 3.0
1993	100,917	+ 9.5	+ 24.6	+ 3.0
1994	111,000	+ 10.0	NA	+ 2.1

Sources: Federal Reserve Bank of Boston, New England Economic Indicators, July, 1994, p. 21; Statistical Abstract of the United States, 1994, Tables 754, 755.

Appendix: External Economies and Diseconomies and the Long-Run Industry Supply Curve

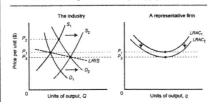

- In a decreasing cost industry, costs decline as a result of industry expansion, and the LRIS is downward-sloping.

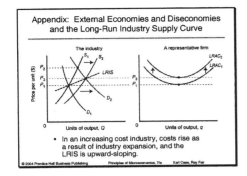

Appendix: External Economies and Diseconomies and the Long-Run Industry Supply Curve

- In an increasing cost industry, costs rise as a result of industry expansion, and the LRIS is upward-sloping.

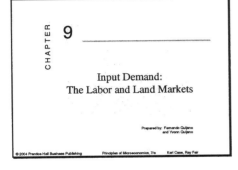

CHAPTER 9

Input Demand:
The Labor and Land Markets

Prepared by: Fernando Quijano
and Yvonn Quijano

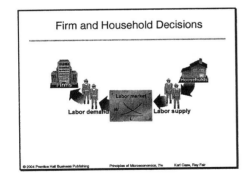

Firm and Household Decisions

Demand for Inputs:
A Derived Demand

- **Derived demand** is demand for resources (inputs) that is dependent on the demand for the outputs those resources can be used to produce.
  - Inputs are demanded by a firm if, and only if, households demand the good or service produced by that firm.

Inputs: Complementary and Substitutable

- The **productivity of an input** is the amount of output produced per unit of that input.
- Inputs can be **complementary** or **substitutable.** This means that a firm's input demands are tightly linked together.

Diminishing Returns

- Faced with a capacity constraint in the short-run, a firm that decides to increase output will eventually encounter diminishing returns.
- **Marginal product of labor (MP_L) is** the additional output produced by one additional unit of labor.

Marginal Revenue Product

- *The marginal revenue product (MRP)* of a variable input is the additional revenue a firm earns by employing one additional unit of input, *ceteris paribus*.

- MRP_L equals the price of output, P_X, times the marginal product of labor, MP_L.

Marginal Revenue Product

Marginal Revenue Product Per Hour of Labor in Sandwich Production (One Grill)

(1) TOTAL LABOR UNITS (EMPLOYEES)	(2) TOTAL PRODUCT (SANDWICHES PER HOUR)	(3) MARGINAL PRODUCT OF LABOR (MP_L) (SANDWICHES PER HOUR)	(4) PRICE (P_X) (VALUE ADDED PER SANDWICH)*	(5) MARGINAL REVENUE PRODUCT ($MP_L \times P_X$) (PER HOUR)
0	0	--	--	--
1	10	10	$ .50	$ 5.00
2	25	15	.50	7.50
3	35	10	.50	5.00
4	40	5	.50	2.50
5	42	2	.50	1.00
6	42	0	.50	0

*The "price" is essentially profit per sandwich; see discussion in text.

Marginal Revenue Product

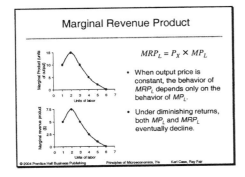

$$MRP_L = P_X \times MP_L$$

- When output price is constant, the behavior of MRP_L depends only on the behavior of MP_L.

- Under diminishing returns, both MP_L and MRP_L eventually decline.

A Firm Using One Variable Factor of Production: Labor

- A competitive firm using only one variable factor of production will use that factor as long as its marginal revenue product exceeds its unit cost.

  - For example, if the firm uses only labor, then it will hire labor as long as MRP_L is greater than the going wage, W^*.

Marginal Revenue Product and Factor Demand for a Firm Using One Variable Input (Labor)

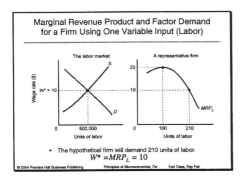

- The hypothetical firm will demand 210 units of labor.
$$W^* = MRP_L = 10$$

Short-Run Demand Curve for a Factor of Production

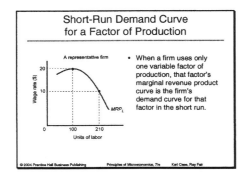

- When a firm uses only one variable factor of production, that factor's marginal revenue product curve is the firm's demand curve for that factor in the short run.

Comparing Marginal Revenue and Marginal Cost to Maximize Profits

- Assuming that labor is the only variable input, if society values a good more than it costs firms to hire the workers to produce that good, the good will be produced.

- Firms weigh the value of outputs as reflected in output price against the value of inputs as reflected in marginal costs.

© 2004 Prentice Hall Business Publishing   Principles of Microeconomics, 7/e   Karl Case, Ray Fair

---

The Two Profit-Maximizing Conditions

- Output prices
- Technology → Marginal revenue product of a unit of input (labor)

Marginal revenue of a unit of output ← Output price

Input prices → Marginal cost of a unit of input (labor)

Marginal cost of a unit of output ← Technology, Input prices

Firm will hire until: Firm will produce until:

$W = MRP_L$ $P = MC$

- The two profit-maximizing conditions are simply two views of the same choice process.

© 2004 Prentice Hall Business Publishing   Principles of Microeconomics, 7/e   Karl Case, Ray Fair

---

The Trade-Off Facing Firms

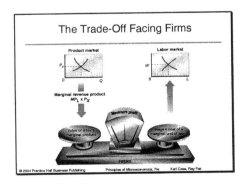

Product market   Labor market

Marginal revenue product
$MP_L \times P_X$

Value of labor's marginal product   Maximum profit   Wage = cost of a marginal unit of labor

FIRMS

© 2004 Prentice Hall Business Publishing   Principles of Microeconomics, 7/e   Karl Case, Ray Fair

A Firm Employing Two Variable Factors of Production in the Short and Long Run

- Land, labor, and capital are used together to produce outputs.

- When an expanding firm adds to its stock of capital, it raises the productivity of its labor, and vice versa. Each factor complements the other.

Substitution and Output Effects of a Change in Factor Price

- Two effects occur when the price of an input changes:

  - *Factor substitution effect:* The tendency of firms to substitute away from a factor whose price has risen and toward a factor whose price has fallen.

Substitution and Output Effects of a Change in Factor Price

- Two effects occur when the price of an input changes:

  - *Output effect of a factor price increase (decrease):* When a firm decreases (increases) its output in response to a factor price increase (decrease), this decreases (increases) its demand for all factors.

Substitution and Output
Effects of a Change in Factor Price

Response of a Firm to an Increasing Wage Rate

TECHNOLOGY	INPUT REQUIREMENTS PER UNIT OF OUTPUT		UNIT COST IF $P_L = \$1$ $P_K = \$1$ $(P_L \times L) + (P_K \times K)$	UNIT COST IF $P_L = \$2$ $P_K = \$1$ $(P_L \times L) + (P_K \times K)$
	K	L		
A (capital intensive)	10	5	$15	$20
B (labor intensive)	3	10	$13	$23

- When $P_L = P_K = \$1$, the labor-intensive method of producing output is less costly.

Substitution and Output
Effects of a Change in Factor Price

The Substitution Effect of an Increase in Wages on a Firm Producing 100 Units of Output

	TO PRODUCE 100 UNITS OF OUTPUT		
	TOTAL CAPITAL DEMANDED	TOTAL LABOR DEMANDED	TOTAL VARIABLE COST
When $P_L = \$1$, $P_K = \$1$, firm uses technology B	300	1,000	$1,300
When $P_L = \$2$, $P_K = \$1$, firm uses technology A	1,000	500	$2,000

- When the price of labor rises, the firm substitutes capital for labor and switches from technique B to technique A.

Many Labor Markets

- If labor markets are competitive, the wages in those markets are determined by the interaction of supply and demand.

- Firms will hire workers only as long as the value of their product exceeds the relevant market wage. This is true in all competitive labor markets.

Land Markets

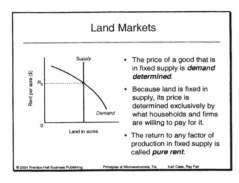

- Unlike labor and capital, the total supply of land is strictly fixed (perfectly inelastic) supply in total.

© 2004 Prentice Hall Business Publishing   Principles of Microeconomics, 7/e   Karl Case, Ray Fair

---

Land Markets

- The price of a good that is in fixed supply is *demand determined*.
- Because land is fixed in supply, its price is determined exclusively by what households and firms are willing to pay for it.
- The return to any factor of production in fixed supply is called *pure rent*.

© 2004 Prentice Hall Business Publishing   Principles of Microeconomics, 7/e   Karl Case, Ray Fair

---

Land Markets

- The supply of land of a *given quality* at a given location is truly fixed in supply.
- The supply of land in a *given use* may not be perfectly inelastic or fixed. As land becomes more valuable for a particular use, people may be willing to pay more and more for it

© 2004 Prentice Hall Business Publishing   Principles of Microeconomics, 7/e   Karl Case, Ray Fair

Rent and the Value of Output Produced on Land

- A firm will pay for and use land as long as the revenue earned from selling the output produced on that land is sufficient to cover the price of the land.

- The firm will use land (A) up to the point at which:

$$MRP_A = P_A$$

The Firm's Profit-Maximization Condition in Input Markets

- The profit-maximizing condition for the perfectly competitive firm in input markets is:

$$P_L = MRP_L = (MP_L \times P_X)$$

$$P_K = MRP_K = (MP_K \times P_X)$$

$$P_A = MRP_A = (MP_A \times P_X)$$

where L is labor, K is capital, A is land (acres), X is output, and P_X is the price of that output.

The Firm's Profit-Maximization Condition in Input Markets

- The profit-maximizing condition for the perfectly competitive firm in input markets, written another way is:

$$\frac{MP_L}{P_L} = \frac{MP_K}{P_K} = \frac{MP_A}{P_A} = \frac{1}{P_X}$$

- In words, the marginal product of the last dollar spent on labor must be equal to the marginal product of the last dollar spent on capital, which must be equal to the marginal product of the last dollar spent on land.

Input Demand Curves

- The factors that can cause factor demand curves to shift include:
  - a change in the demand for outputs,
  - a change in the quantity of complementary or substitutable inputs,
  - changes in the prices of other inputs, and
  - technological change

Shifts in Factor Demand Curves

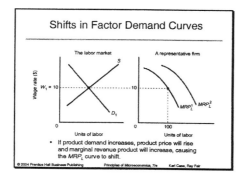

- If product demand increases, product price will rise and marginal revenue product will increase, causing the MRP_L curve to shift.

Input Demand Curves

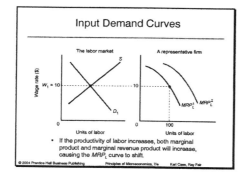

- If the productivity of labor increases, both marginal product and marginal revenue product will increase, causing the MRP_L curve to shift.

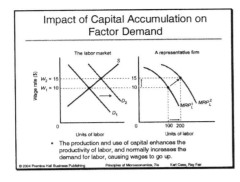

Impact of Capital Accumulation on Factor Demand

- The production and use of capital enhances the productivity of labor, and normally increases the demand for labor, causing wages to go up.

Impact of Technological Change

- *Technological change* refers to the introduction of new methods of production or new products intended to increase the productivity of existing inputs or to raise marginal products.

- Technological change can, and does, have a powerful influence on factor demands.

Resource Allocation and the Mix of Output in Competitive Markets

- We have studied the fundamental decisions that perfectly competitive, profit-maximizing firms must make in both output and input markets.

- The distribution of income among households is determined by factor productivity as measured by marginal revenue product. This is referred to as the *marginal productivity theory of income distribution*.

Review Terms and Concepts

demand-determined price

derived demand

factor substitution effect

marginal product of labor (MP_L)

marginal productivity theory of income distribution

marginal revenue product (MRP_L)

output effect of a factor price increase (decrease)

productivity of an input

pure rent

technological change

© 2004 Prentice Hall Business Publishing   Principles of Microeconomics, 7/e   Karl Case, Ray Fair

---

CHAPTER 10

Input Demand:
The Capital Market and
the Investment Decision

Appendix: Calculating Present Value

Prepared by Fernando Quijano
and Yvonn Quijano

© 2004 Prentice Hall Business Publishing   Principles of Microeconomics, 7/e   Karl Case, Ray Fair

---

The Capital Market

© 2004 Prentice Hall Business Publishing   Principles of Microeconomics, 7/e   Karl Case, Ray Fair

Capital

- *Capital* are those goods produced by the economic system that are used as inputs to produce other goods and services in the future.

Tangible Capital

- *Physical*, or *tangible*, *capital* refers to the material things used as inputs in the production of future goods and services.
- Major categories of physical capital are:
  - Nonresidential structures
  - Durable equipment
  - Residential structures
  - Inventories

Social Capital: Infrastructure

- *Social capital*, or *infrastructure*, is capital that provides services to the public.
- Most social capital takes the form of:
  - Public works (roads and bridges)
  - Public services (police and fire protection)

Intangible Capital

- *Intangible capital* refers to nonmaterial things that contribute to the output of future goods and services.

- For example, an advertising campaign to establish a brand name produces intangible capital called goodwill.

Intangible Capital

- *Human capital* is a form of intangible capital that includes the skills and other knowledge that workers have or acquire through education and training.

- Human capital yields valuable services to a firm over time.

Measuring Capital

- The measure of a firm's *capital stock* is the current market value of its plant, equipment, inventories, and intangible assets.

- When we speak of capital, we refer not to money or financial assets such as bonds or stocks, but to the firm's physical plant, equipment, inventory, and intangible assets.

Investment and Depreciation

- *Investment* refers to new capital additions to a firm's capital stock.
  - Although capital is measured at a given point in time (a stock), investment is measured over a period of time (a flow).
  - The flow of investment increases the capital stock.
- *Depreciation* is a decline in an asset's economic value over time.

Private Investment in the U.S. Economy, 2002

	BILLIONS OF CURRENT DOLLARS	AS A PERCENTAGE OF TOTAL GROSS INVESTMENT	AS A PERCENTAGE OF GDP
Nonresidential structures	269.3	16.9	2.6
Equipment and software	848.1	53.2	8.1
Change in inventories	3.9	0.2	0.0
Residential structures and equipment	471.9	29.6	4.5
Total gross private investment	1593.2	100.0	15.2
– depreciation	– 1393.5	– 87.5	– 13.3
Net investment =	199.7	12.5	1.9%
gross investment minus depreciation			

The Capital Market

- The *capital market* is a market in which households supply their savings to firms that demand funds to buy capital goods.

The Capital Market

$1,000 in savings becomes $1,000 of investment

The Capital Market

- A *bond* is a contract between a borrower and a lender, in which the borrower agrees to pay the loan at some time in the future, along with interest payments along the way.

- The *financial capital market* is the part of the capital market in which savers and investors interact through intermediaries.

Capital Income: Interest and Profits

- *Capital income* is income earned on savings that have been put to use through financial capital markets.

- *Interest* is the payment made for the use of money. Interest is a reward for postponing consumption.

- *Profit* is the excess of revenues over cost in a given period. Profit is a reward for innovation and risk taking.

Financial Markets in Action

- Four mechanisms for channeling household savings into investment projects include:
  - Business loans
  - Venture capital
  - Retained earnings
  - The stock market

© 2004 Prentice Hall Business Publishing   Principles of Microeconomics, 7/e   Karl Case, Ray Fair

Financial Markets Link Household Saving and Investment by Firms

© 2004 Prentice Hall Business Publishing   Principles of Microeconomics, 7/e   Karl Case, Ray Fair

Capital Accumulation and Allocation

- In modern industrial societies, investment decisions (capital production decisions) are made primarily by firms.
- Households decide how much to save, and in the long-run saving limits or constrains the amount of investment that firms can undertake. The capital market exists to direct savings into profitable investment projects.

© 2004 Prentice Hall Business Publishing   Principles of Microeconomics, 7/e   Karl Case, Ray Fair

The Demand for New Capital and the Investment Decision

- Decision makers must have *expectations* about what is going to happen in the future.

- The investment process requires that the potential investor evaluate the expected flow of future productive services that an investment project will yield.

Forming Expectations

- The ability to lend at the market rate of interest means that there is an *opportunity cost* associated with every investment project.

- The evaluation process thus involves not only estimating *future benefits*, but also comparing the possible *alternative uses* of the funds required to undertake the project. At a minimum, those funds earn interest in financial markets.

Comparing Costs and Expected Return

- The *expected rate of return* is the annual rate of return that a firm expects to obtain through a capital investment.

Comparing Costs and Expected Return

- The expected rate of return on an investment project depends on:
  - the price of the investment,
  - the expected length of time the project provides additional cost savings or revenue, and
  - the expected amount of revenue attributable each year to the project.

© 2004 Prentice Hall Business Publishing   Principles of Microeconomics, 7/e   Karl Case, Ray Fair

Comparing Costs and Expected Return

Potential Investment Projects and Expected Rates of Return for a Hypothetical Firm, Based on Forecasts of Future Profits Attributable to the Investment

PROJECT	(1) TOTAL INVESTMENT (DOLLARS)	(2) EXPECTED RATE OF RETURN (PERCENT)
A. New computer network	400,000	25
B. New branch plant	2,600,000	20
C. Sales office in another state	1,500,000	15
D. New automated billing system	100,000	12
E. Ten new delivery trucks	400,000	10
F. Advertising campaign	1,000,000	7
G. Employee cafeteria	100,000	5

© 2004 Prentice Hall Business Publishing   Principles of Microeconomics, 7/e   Karl Case, Ray Fair

Investment as a Function of the Market Interest Rate

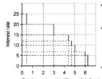

- The demand for new capital depends on the interest rate.
- When the interest rate is low firms are more likely to invest in new plant and equipment.
- The interest rate determines the opportunity cost (alternative investment) of each project.

© 2004 Prentice Hall Business Publishing   Principles of Microeconomics, 7/e   Karl Case, Ray Fair

Investment Demand

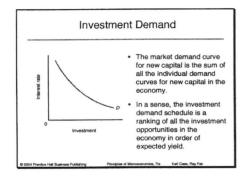

- The market demand curve for new capital is the sum of all the individual demand curves for new capital in the economy.

- In a sense, the investment demand schedule is a ranking of all the investment opportunities in the economy in order of expected yield.

The Expected Rate of Return and the Marginal Revenue Product of Capital

- A perfectly competitive profit-maximizing firm will keep investing in new capital up to the point at which the expected rate of return is equal to the interest rate.

- This is analogous to:

$$MRP_K = P_K$$

Review Terms and Concepts

Bond	Human capital
Capital	Intangible capital
Capital income	Interest
Capital market	Investment
Capital stock	Physical, or tangible, capital
Depreciation	Profit
Expected rate of return	Social capital, or infrastructure
Financial capital market	

Appendix:
Calculating Present Value

Expected Profits from a $1,200 Investment Project	
Year 1	$100
Year 2	100
Year 3	400
Year 4	500
Year 5	500
All later years	0
Total	1,600

- Based on the expected profits as listed and the cost of $1,200, should the investment project be undertaken?

Appendix:
Calculating Present Value

- Present-value analysis is a method of evaluating future revenue streams.
- The "price" (X) of $1 to be delivered a year from now with interest (r) equals:

$$X + rX = X(1 + r)$$

$$\$1 = X(1 + r), \text{ so } X = \frac{\$1}{1 + r}$$

Appendix:
Calculating Present Value

- The present value of $100 to be delivered in two years at an annual interest rate of 10 percent equals:

$$X = \frac{\$100}{(1.1)^2} = \$82.64$$

- $82.64 plus interest of $8.26 after one year and interest of $9.09 in the second year would leave you with $100 at the end of two years.

Appendix: Calculating Present Value

- In general, the present value (*PV*), or present discounted value, of *R* dollars *t* years from now is:

$$PV = \frac{R}{(1+r)^t}$$

Appendix: Calculating Present Value

Calculation of Total Present Value of a Hypothetical Investment Project (Assuming *r* = 10 Percent)

END OF...	$(R)	DIVIDED BY (1 + r)^t	=	PRESENT VALUE ($)
Year 1	100	(1.1)		90.91
Year 2	100	$(1.1)^2$		82.65
Year 3	400	$(1.1)^3$		300.53
Year 4	500	$(1.1)^4$		341.51
Year 5	500	$(1.1)^5$		310.46
Total Present Value				1,126.06

- An investment project with an initial outlay of $1,200 and a PV = $1,126.06 based on r = 10% would not be undertaken.

Appendix: Calculating Present Value

- Lower interest rates result in higher present values. The firm has to *pay more now* to purchase the same number of future dollars.

$100
10%
2 years
$$X = \frac{\$100}{(1.1)^2} = \$82.64$$

$100
5%
2 years
$$X = \frac{\$100}{(1+r)^2} = \frac{\$100}{(1.05)^2} = \$90.70$$

Appendix: Calculating Present Value

Calculation of Total Present Value of a Hypothetical Investment Project (Assuming r = 5 Percent)

END OF...	(R)	DIVIDED BY $(1 + r)^t$ =	PRESENT VALUE ($)
Year 1	100	(1.05)	95.24
Year 2	100	$(1.05)^2$	90.70
Year 3	400	$(1.05)^3$	345.54
Year 4	500	$(1.05)^4$	411.35
Year 5	500	$(1.05)^5$	391.76
Total Present Value			1,334.59

- An investment project with an initial outlay of $1,200 and a PV = $1,334.59 based on r = 5% should be undertaken.

© 2004 Prentice Hall Business Publishing   Principles of Microeconomics, 7/e   Karl Case, Ray Fair

Appendix: Calculating Present Value

- The basic rule is:
  - If the present value of an expected stream of earnings from an investment is greater (less) than the cost of the investment necessary to undertake it, then the investment should (should not) be undertaken.

© 2004 Prentice Hall Business Publishing   Principles of Microeconomics, 7/e   Karl Case, Ray Fair

CHAPTER 10

Input Demand: The Capital Market and the Investment Decision

Appendix: Calculating Present Value

Prepared by Fernando Quijano and Yvonn Quijano

© 2004 Prentice Hall Business Publishing   Principles of Microeconomics, 7/e   Karl Case, Ray Fair

The Capital Market

© 2004 Prentice Hall Business Publishing   Principles of Microeconomics, 7/e   Karl Case, Ray Fair

Capital

- *Capital* are those goods produced by the economic system that are used as inputs to produce other goods and services in the future.

© 2004 Prentice Hall Business Publishing   Principles of Microeconomics, 7/e   Karl Case, Ray Fair

Tangible Capital

- *Physical*, or *tangible*, *capital* refers to the material things used as inputs in the production of future goods and services.
- Major categories of physical capital are:
  - Nonresidential structures
  - Durable equipment
  - Residential structures
  - Inventories

© 2004 Prentice Hall Business Publishing   Principles of Microeconomics, 7/e   Karl Case, Ray Fair

Social Capital: Infrastructure

- *Social capital*, or *infrastructure*, is capital that provides services to the public.
- Most social capital takes the form of:
  - Public works (roads and bridges)
  - Public services (police and fire protection)

Intangible Capital

- *Intangible capital* refers to nonmaterial things that contribute to the output of future goods and services.
- For example, an advertising campaign to establish a brand name produces intangible capital called goodwill.

Intangible Capital

- *Human capital* is a form of intangible capital that includes the skills and other knowledge that workers have or acquire through education and training.
- Human capital yields valuable services to a firm over time.

Measuring Capital

- The measure of a firm's *capital stock* is the current market value of its plant, equipment, inventories, and intangible assets.
- When we speak of capital, we refer not to money or financial assets such as bonds or stocks, but to the firm's physical plant, equipment, inventory, and intangible assets.

Investment and Depreciation

- *Investment* refers to new capital additions to a firm's capital stock.
  - Although capital is measured at a given point in time (a stock), investment is measured over a period of time (a flow).
  - The flow of investment increases the capital stock.
- *Depreciation* is a decline in an asset's economic value over time.

Private Investment in the U.S. Economy, 2002

	BILLIONS OF CURRENT DOLLARS	AS A PERCENTAGE OF TOTAL GROSS INVESTMENT	AS A PERCENTAGE OF GDP
Nonresidential structures	269.3	16.9	2.6
Equipment and software	848.1	53.2	8.1
Change in inventories	3.9	0.2	0.0
Residential structures and equipment	471.9	29.6	4.5
Total gross private investment	1593.2	100.0	15.2
- depreciation	-1393.5	-87.5	-13.3
Net investment =	199.7	12.5	1.9%
gross investment minus depreciation			

The Capital Market

- The *capital market* is a market in which households supply their savings to firms that demand funds to buy capital goods.

The Capital Market

$1,000 in savings becomes $1,000 of investment

The Capital Market

- A *bond* is a contract between a borrower and a lender, in which the borrower agrees to pay the loan at some time in the future, along with interest payments along the way.

- The *financial capital market* is the part of the capital market in which savers and investors interact through intermediaries.

Capital Income: Interest and Profits

- *Capital income* is income earned on savings that have been put to use through financial capital markets.

- *Interest* is the payment made for the use of money. Interest is a reward for postponing consumption.

- *Profit* is the excess of revenues over cost in a given period. Profit is a reward for innovation and risk taking.

© 2004 Prentice Hall Business Publishing Principles of Microeconomics, 7/e Karl Case, Ray Fair

Financial Markets in Action

- Four mechanisms for channeling household savings into investment projects include:
  - Business loans
  - Venture capital
  - Retained earnings
  - The stock market

© 2004 Prentice Hall Business Publishing Principles of Microeconomics, 7/e Karl Case, Ray Fair

Financial Markets Link Household Saving and Investment by Firms

© 2004 Prentice Hall Business Publishing Principles of Microeconomics, 7/e Karl Case, Ray Fair

Capital Accumulation and Allocation

- In modern industrial societies, investment decisions (capital production decisions) are made primarily by firms.

- Households decide how much to save, and in the long-run saving limits or constrains the amount of investment that firms can undertake. The capital market exists to direct savings into profitable investment projects.

The Demand for New Capital and the Investment Decision

- Decision makers must have *expectations* about what is going to happen in the future.

- The investment process requires that the potential investor evaluate the expected flow of future productive services that an investment project will yield.

Forming Expectations

- The ability to lend at the market rate of interest means that there is an *opportunity cost* associated with every investment project.

- The evaluation process thus involves not only estimating *future benefits*, but also comparing the possible *alternative uses* of the funds required to undertake the project. At a minimum, those funds earn interest in financial markets.

Comparing Costs and Expected Return

- The *expected rate of return* is the annual rate of return that a firm expects to obtain through a capital investment.

Comparing Costs and Expected Return

- The expected rate of return on an investment project depends on:
  - the price of the investment,
  - the expected length of time the project provides additional cost savings or revenue, and
  - the expected amount of revenue attributable each year to the project.

Comparing Costs and Expected Return

Potential Investment Projects and Expected Rates of Return for a Hypothetical Firm, Based on Forecasts of Future Profits Attributable to the Investment

PROJECT	(1) TOTAL INVESTMENT (DOLLARS)	(2) EXPECTED RATE OF RETURN (PERCENT)
A. New computer network	400,000	25
B. New branch plant	2,800,000	20
C. Sales office in another state	1,500,000	15
D. New automated billing system	100,000	12
E. Ten new delivery trucks	400,000	10
F. Advertising campaign	1,000,000	7
G. Employee cafeteria	100,000	5

Investment as a Function of the Market Interest Rate

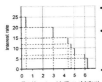

- The demand for new capital depends on the interest rate.
- When the interest rate is low firms are more likely to invest in new plant and equipment.
- The interest rate determines the opportunity cost (alternative investment) of each project.

Investment Demand

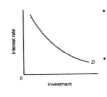

- The market demand curve for new capital is the sum of all the individual demand curves for new capital in the economy.
- In a sense, the investment demand schedule is a ranking of all the investment opportunities in the economy in order of expected yield.

The Expected Rate of Return and the Marginal Revenue Product of Capital

- A perfectly competitive profit-maximizing firm will keep investing in new capital up to the point at which the expected rate of return is equal to the interest rate.
- This is analogous to:

$$MRP_K = P_K$$

Review Terms and Concepts

Bond	Human capital
Capital	Intangible capital
Capital income	Interest
Capital market	Investment
Capital stock	Physical, or tangible, capital
Depreciation	Profit
Expected rate of return	Social capital, or infrastructure
Financial capital market	

© 2004 Prentice Hall Business Publishing   Principles of Microeconomics, 7/e   Karl Case, Ray Fair

---

Appendix: Calculating Present Value

Expected Profits from a $1,200 Investment Project

Year 1	$100
Year 2	100
Year 3	400
Year 4	500
Year 5	500
All later years	0
Total	1,600

- Based on the expected profits as listed and the cost of $1,200, should the investment project be undertaken?

© 2004 Prentice Hall Business Publishing   Principles of Microeconomics, 7/e   Karl Case, Ray Fair

---

Appendix: Calculating Present Value

- Present-value analysis is a method of evaluating future revenue streams.

- The "price" (X) of $1 to be delivered a year from now with interest (r) equals:

$$X + rX = X(1+r)$$

$$\$1 = X(1+r), \text{ so } X = \frac{\$1}{1+r}$$

© 2004 Prentice Hall Business Publishing   Principles of Microeconomics, 7/e   Karl Case, Ray Fair

Appendix:
Calculating Present Value

- The present value of $100 to be delivered in two years at an annual interest rate of 10 percent equals:

$$X = \frac{\$100}{(1.1)^2} = \$82.64$$

- $82.64 plus interest of $8.26 after one year and interest of $9.09 in the second year would leave you with $100 at the end of two years.

Appendix:
Calculating Present Value

- In general, the present value (PV), or present discounted value, of R dollars t years from now is:

$$PV = \frac{R}{(1+r)^t}$$

Appendix:
Calculating Present Value

Calculation of Total Present Value of a Hypothetical Investment Project (Assuming r = 10 Percent)

END OF...	$(R)	DIVIDED BY $(1 + r)^t$ =	PRESENT VALUE ($)
Year 1	100	(1.1)	90.91
Year 2	100	$(1.1)^2$	82.65
Year 3	400	$(1.1)^3$	300.53
Year 4	500	$(1.1)^4$	341.51
Year 5	500	$(1.1)^5$	310.46
Total Present Value			1,126.06

- An investment project with an initial outlay of $1,200 and a PV = $1,126.06 based on r = 10% would not be undertaken.

Appendix: Calculating Present Value

- Lower interest rates result in higher present values. The firm has to *pay more now* to purchase the same number of future dollars.

$100
10%
2 years
$$X = \frac{\$100}{(1.1)^2} = \$82.64$$

$100
5%
2 years
$$X = \frac{\$100}{(1+r)^2} = \frac{\$100}{(1.05)^2} = \$90.70$$

Appendix: Calculating Present Value

Calculation of Total Present Value of a Hypothetical Investment Project (Assuming r = 5 Percent)

END OF...	$(R)	DIVIDED BY $(1 + r)^t$ =	PRESENT VALUE ($)
Year 1	100	(1.05)	95.24
Year 2	100	$(1.05)^2$	90.70
Year 3	400	$(1.05)^3$	345.54
Year 4	500	$(1.05)^4$	411.35
Year 5	500	$(1.05)^5$	391.76
Total Present Value			1,334.59

- An investment project with an initial outlay of $1,200 and a PV = $1,334.59 based on r = 5% should be undertaken.

Appendix: Calculating Present Value

- The basic rule is:

  - If the present value of an expected stream of earnings from an investment is greater (less) than the cost of the investment necessary to undertake it, then the investment should (should not) be undertaken.

CHAPTER 11

General Equilibrium
and the Efficiency
of Perfect Competition

Prepared by: Fernando Quijano
and Yvonn Quijano

© 2004 Prentice Hall Business Publishing   Principles of Microeconomics, 7/e   Karl Case, Ray Fair

---

Firm and Household Decisions

- Input and output markets cannot be considered separately or as if they operated independently.

© 2004 Prentice Hall Business Publishing   Principles of Microeconomics, 7/e   Karl Case, Ray Fair

---

General Equilibrium and the Efficiency of Perfect Competition

- *Partial equilibrium analysis* is the process of examining the equilibrium conditions in individual markets and for households and firms separately.

- *General equilibrium* is the condition that exists when all markets in an economy are in simultaneous equilibrium.

© 2004 Prentice Hall Business Publishing   Principles of Microeconomics, 7/e   Karl Case, Ray Fair

General Equilibrium and the Efficiency of Perfect Competition

- In judging the performance of an economic system, two criteria used are efficiency and equity (fairness).

- *Efficiency* is the condition in which the economy is producing what people want at the least possible cost.

General Equilibrium Analysis

- To examine the move from partial to general equilibrium analysis we will consider the impact of:

  - a major technological advance, and
  - a shift in consumer preferences.

A Technological Advance: The Electronic Calculator

- Technology improvements made it possible to produce at lower costs in the calculator industry.

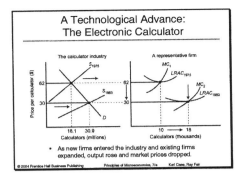

A Technological Advance: The Electronic Calculator

- As new firms entered the industry and existing firms expanded, output rose and market prices dropped.

© 2004 Prentice Hall Business Publishing · Principles of Microeconomics, 7/e · Karl Case, Ray Fair

---

A Technological Advance: The Electronic Calculator

- A significant technological change in a single industry affects many markets:
  - Households face a different structure of prices and must adjust their consumption of many products.
  - Labor reacts to new skill requirements and is reallocated across markets.
  - Capital is also reallocated.

© 2004 Prentice Hall Business Publishing · Principles of Microeconomics, 7/e · Karl Case, Ray Fair

---

A Shift in Consumer Preferences: The Wine Industry in the 1970s

- To examine the effects of a change in one market on other markets, we will consider the wine industry in the 1970s.

Production and Consumption of Wine in the United States, 1965–1980

YEAR	U.S. PRODUCTION (MILLIONS OF GALLONS)	IMPORTS (MILLIONS OF GALLONS)	TOTAL (MILLIONS OF GALLONS)	CONSUMPTION PER CAPITA (GALLONS)
1965	565	10	575	1.32
1970	713	22	735	1.52
1975	782	40	822	1.96
1980	983	91	1073	2.02
Percent change, 1965–1980	+ 74.0	+ 810.0	+ 86.6	+ 53.0

Source: U.S. Department of Commerce, Bureau of the Census, Statistical Abstract of the United States, 1985, Table 1364, p. 765.

© 2004 Prentice Hall Business Publishing · Principles of Microeconomics, 7/e · Karl Case, Ray Fair

Adjustment in an Economy with Two Sectors

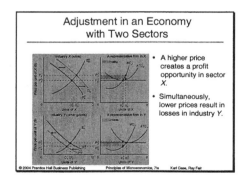

- This graph shows the initial equilibrium in an economy with two sectors—wine (X) and other goods (Y)—prior to a change in consumer preferences.

Adjustment in an Economy with Two Sectors

- A change in consumer preferences causes an increase in the demand for wine, and, consequently, a decrease in the demand for other goods.

Adjustment in an Economy with Two Sectors

- A higher price creates a profit opportunity in sector X.
- Simultaneously, lower prices result in losses in industry Y.

Adjustment in an Economy with Two Sectors

- As new firms enter industry *X* and existing firms expand, output rises and market prices drop. Excess profits are eliminated.

© 2004 Prentice Hall Business Publishing   Principles of Microeconomics, 7/e   Karl Case, Ray Fair

---

Adjustment in an Economy with Two Sectors

- As new firms exit industry *Y,* market price rises and losses are eliminated.

© 2004 Prentice Hall Business Publishing   Principles of Microeconomics, 7/e   Karl Case, Ray Fair

---

A Shift in Consumer Preferences: The Wine Industry in the 1970s

Land in Grape Production in the United States and in California Alone, 1974 and 1982		
	NUMBER OF VINEYARDS	NUMBER OF ACRES
United States		
1974	14,208	712,804
1982	24,982	874,996
Percent change	+ 75.8	+ 22.8
California		
1974	8,333	607,011
1982	10,481	756,720
Percent change	+ 25.8	+ 24.7

Source: U.S. Department of Commerce, Bureau of the Census, Census of Agriculture (1974 and 1982), 1, part 51.

© 2004 Prentice Hall Business Publishing   Principles of Microeconomics, 7/e   Karl Case, Ray Fair

Formal Proof of a
General Competitive Equilibrium

- This section explains why perfect competition is efficient in dividing scarce resources among alternative uses.

- If the assumptions of a perfectly competitive economic system hold, the economy will produce an efficient allocation of resources.

Pareto Efficiency

- *Pareto efficiency,* or *Pareto optimality,* is a condition in which no change is possible that will make some members of society better off without making some other members of society worse off.

- This very precise concept of efficiency is known as *allocative efficiency.*

The Efficiency of Perfect Competition

- The three basic questions in a competitive economy are:

    1. *What will be produced?* What determines the final mix of output?

    2. *How will it be produced?* How do capital, labor, and land get divided up among firms?

    3. *Who will get what is produced?* What is the distribution of output among consuming households?

The Efficiency of Perfect Competition

- As we will see, in a perfectly competitive economic system:

  1. resources are allocated among firms efficiently,
  2. final products are distributed among households efficiently, and
  3. the system produces the things that people want.

The Efficiency of Perfect Competition

Efficient Allocation of Resources:

- Perfectly competitive firms have incentives to use the best available technology.
- With a full knowledge of existing technologies, firms will choose the technology that produces the output they want at the least cost.
- Each firm uses inputs such that $MRP_L = P_L$. The marginal value of each input to each firm is just equal to its market price.

The Efficiency of Perfect Competition

Efficient Distribution of Outputs Among Households:

- Within the constraints imposed by income and wealth, households are free to choose among all the goods and services available in output markets. Utility value is revealed in market behavior.
- As long as everyone shops freely in the same markets, no redistribution of final outputs among people will make them better off.

The Efficiency of Perfect Competition

Producing What People Want—the Efficient Mix of Output:

- Society will produce the efficient mix of output if all firms equate price and marginal cost.

Principles of Microeconomics, 7/e   Karl Case, Ray Fair

The Key Efficiency Condition: Price Equals Marginal Cost

If $P_X > MC_X$, society gains value by producing more X

If $P_X < MC_X$, society gains value by producing

The value placed on good X by society through the market, or the social value of a marginal unit of X.

P_X = MC_X

Market-determined value of resources needed to produce a marginal unit of X. MC_X is equal to the opportunity cost of those resources, lost production of other goods or the value of the resources left unemployed (leisure, vacant land, etc).

Principles of Microeconomics, 7/e   Karl Case, Ray Fair

Efficiency in Perfect Competition

- Efficiency in perfect competition follows from a weighing of values by both households and firms.

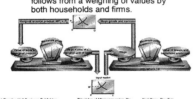

Principles of Microeconomics, 7/e   Karl Case, Ray Fair

The Sources of Market Failure

- *Market failure* occurs when resources are misallocated, or allocated inefficiently. The result is waste or lost value. Evidence of market failure is revealed by the existence of:
  - Imperfect market structure
  - Public goods
  - External costs and benefits
  - Imperfect information

Imperfect Markets

- *Imperfect competition* is an industry in which single firms have some control over price and competition. Imperfectly competitive industries give rise to an inefficient allocation of resources.

Imperfect Markets

- *Monopoly* is an industry composed of only one firm that produces a product for which there are no close substitutes and in which significant barriers exist to prevent new firms from entering the industry.

Imperfect Markets

- In all imperfectly competitive industries, output is lower—the product is underproduced—and price is higher than it would be under perfect competition.

  - The equilibrium condition $P = MC$ does not hold, and the system does not produce the most efficient product mix.

Public Goods

- *Public goods*, or *social goods* are goods and services that bestow collective benefits on members of society.

  - Generally, no one can be excluded from enjoying their benefits. The classic example is national defense.

Public Goods

- *Private goods* are products produced by firms for sale to individual households.

  - Private provision of public goods fails. A completely laissez-faire market will not produce everything that all members of a society might want. Citizens must band together to ensure that desired public goods are produced, and this is generally accomplished through government spending financed by taxes.

Externalities

- An **externality** is a cost or benefit resulting from some activity or transaction that is imposed or bestowed on parties outside the activity or transaction.
  - The market does not always force consideration of all the costs and benefits of decisions. Yet for an economy to achieve an efficient allocation of resources, all costs and benefits must be weighed.

© 2004 Prentice Hall Business Publishing   Principles of Microeconomics, 7/e   Karl Case, Ray Fair

Imperfect Information

- **Imperfect information** is the absence of full knowledge concerning product characteristics, available prices, and so forth.
  - The absence of full information can lead to transactions that are ultimately disadvantageous.

© 2004 Prentice Hall Business Publishing   Principles of Microeconomics, 7/e   Karl Case, Ray Fair

Review Terms and Concepts

efficiency
externality
general equilibrium
imperfect competition
imperfect information
market failure

monopoly
Pareto efficiency, or Pareto optimality
partial equilibrium analysis
private goods
public goods, or social goods

© 2004 Prentice Hall Business Publishing   Principles of Microeconomics, 7/e   Karl Case, Ray Fair

---

CHAPTER 12

Monopoly
and Antitrust Policy

Prepared by: Fernando Quijano
and Yvonn Quijano

Imperfect Competition and Market Power: Core Concepts

- An *imperfectly competitive industry* is an industry in which single firms have some control over the price of their output.

- *Market power* is the imperfectly competitive firm's ability to raise price without losing all demand for its product.

Defining Industry Boundaries

- The ease with which consumers can substitute for a product limits the extent to which a monopolist can exercise market power.

- The more broadly a market is defined, the more difficult it becomes to find substitutes.

Pure Monopoly

- A *pure monopoly* is an industry with a single firm that produces a product for which there are no close substitutes and in which significant barriers to entry prevent other firms from entering the industry to compete for profits.

© 2004 Prentice Hall Business Publishing   Principles of Microeconomics, 7/e   Karl Case, Ray Fair

Barriers to Entry

- A *barrier to entry* is something that prevents new firms from entering and competing in imperfectly competitive industries.

© 2004 Prentice Hall Business Publishing   Principles of Microeconomics, 7/e   Karl Case, Ray Fair

Barriers to Entry

- Barriers to entry include:
  - *Government franchises*, or firms that become monopolies by virtue of a government directive.

© 2004 Prentice Hall Business Publishing   Principles of Microeconomics, 7/e   Karl Case, Ray Fair

Barriers to Entry

- Barriers to entry include:
  - *Patents* or barriers that grant the exclusive use of the patented product or process to the inventor.

Barriers to Entry

- Barriers to entry include:
  - *Economies of scale and other cost advantages* enjoyed by industries that have large capital requirements. A large initial investment, or the need to embark in an expensive advertising campaign, deter would-be entrants to the industry.

Barriers to Entry

- Barriers to entry include:
  - *Ownership of a scarce factor of production:* If production requires a particular input, and one firm owns the entire supply of that input, that firm will control the industry.

Price: The Fourth Decision Variable

- Firms with market power must decide:
    1. how much to produce,
    2. how to produce it,
    3. how much to demand in each input market, and
    4. **what price to charge for their output.**

Price and Output Decisions in Pure Monopoly Markets

- To analyze monopoly behavior we assume that:
    - Entry to the market is blocked
    - Firms act to maximize profit
    - The pure monopolist buys inputs in competitive input markets
    - The monopolistic firm cannot price discriminate
    - The monopoly faces a known demand curve

Price and Output Decisions in Pure Monopoly Markets

- In a monopoly market, there is no distinction between the firm and the industry because the firm is the industry.
- The market demand curve is the demand curve facing the firm, and total quantity supplied in the market is what the firm decides to produce.

Price and Output Decisions in Pure Monopoly Markets

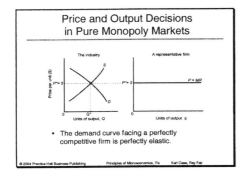

- The demand curve facing a perfectly competitive firm is perfectly elastic.

© 2004 Prentice Hall Business Publishing   Principles of Microeconomics, 7/e   Karl Case, Ray Fair

Marginal Revenue Facing a Monopolist

Marginal Revenue Facing a Monopolist

(1) QUANTITY	(2) PRICE	(3) TOTAL REVENUE	(4) MARGINAL REVENUE
0	$11	0	–
1	10	$10	$10
2	9	18	8
3	8	24	6
4	7	28	4
5	6	30	2
6	5	30	0
7	4	28	−2
8	3	24	−4
9	2	18	−6
10	1	10	−8

© 2004 Prentice Hall Business Publishing   Principles of Microeconomics, 7/e   Karl Case, Ray Fair

Marginal Revenue and Market Demand

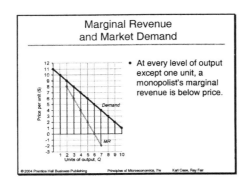

- At every level of output except one unit, a monopolist's marginal revenue is below price.

© 2004 Prentice Hall Business Publishing   Principles of Microeconomics, 7/e   Karl Case, Ray Fair

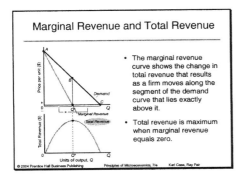

Marginal Revenue and Total Revenue

- The marginal revenue curve shows the change in total revenue that results as a firm moves along the segment of the demand curve that lies exactly above it.

- Total revenue is maximum when marginal revenue equals zero.

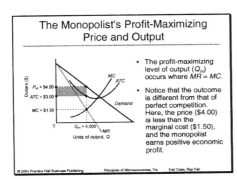

The Monopolist's Profit-Maximizing Price and Output

- The profit-maximizing level of output (Q_m) occurs where $MR = MC$.

- Notice that the outcome is different from that of perfect competition. Here, the price ($4.00) is less than the marginal cost ($1.50), and the monopolist earns positive economic profit.

The Absence of a Supply Curve in Monopoly

- A monopoly firm has no supply curve that is independent of the demand curve for its product.

- A monopolist sets both price and quantity, and the amount of output supplied depends on both its marginal cost curve and the demand curve that it faces.

Monopoly in the Long and Short-Run

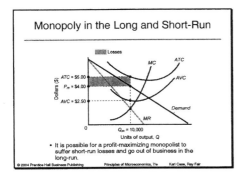

- It is possible for a profit-maximizing monopolist to suffer short-run losses and go out of business in the long-run.

© 2004 Prentice Hall Business Publishing   Principles of Microeconomics, 7/e   Karl Case, Ray Fair

Perfect Competition and Monopoly Compared

- In a perfectly competitive industry in the long-run, price will be equal to long-run average cost.

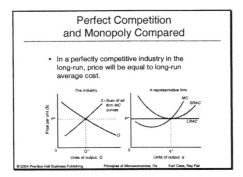

© 2004 Prentice Hall Business Publishing   Principles of Microeconomics, 7/e   Karl Case, Ray Fair

Perfect Competition and Monopoly Compared

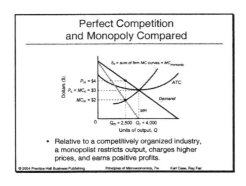

- Relative to a competitively organized industry, a monopolist restricts output, charges higher prices, and earns positive profits.

© 2004 Prentice Hall Business Publishing   Principles of Microeconomics, 7/e   Karl Case, Ray Fair

Collusion and Monopoly Compared

- *Collusion* is the act of working with other producers in an effort to limit competition and increase joint profits.

- When firms collude, the outcome would be exactly the same as the outcome of a monopoly in the industry.

The Social Costs of Monopoly

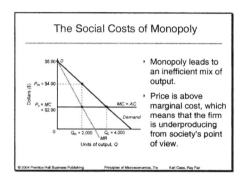

- Monopoly leads to an inefficient mix of output.

- Price is above marginal cost, which means that the firm is underproducing from society's point of view.

The Social Costs of Monopoly

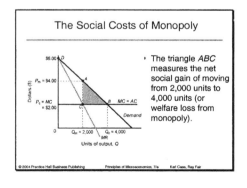

- The triangle *ABC* measures the net social gain of moving from 2,000 units to 4,000 units (or welfare loss from monopoly).

Rent-Seeking Behavior

Rent-seeking behavior refers to actions taken to preserve positive profits.

A rational owner would be willing to pay any amount less than the entire green rectangle to prevent those positive profits from being eliminated as a result of entry.

Government Failure

- The idea of rent-seeking behavior introduces the notion of *government failure*, in which the government becomes the tool of the rent-seeker, and the allocation of resources is made even less efficient than before.

Public Choice Theory

- The idea of government failure is at the center of *public choice theory*, which holds that public officials who set economic policies and regulate the players act in their own self-interest, just as firms do.

Price Discrimination

- Charging different prices to different buyers is called *price discrimination*.

- A firm that charges the maximum amount that buyers are willing to pay for each unit is practicing *perfect price discrimination*.

Price Discrimination

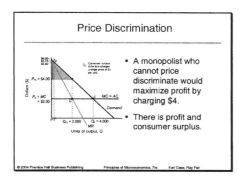

- A monopolist who cannot price discriminate would maximize profit by charging $4.

- There is profit and consumer surplus.

Price Discrimination

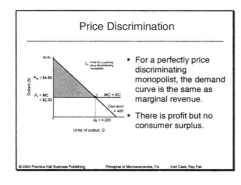

- For a perfectly price discriminating monopolist, the demand curve is the same as marginal revenue.

- There is profit but no consumer surplus.

Remedies for Monopoly: Antitrust Policy

- A *trust* is an arrangement in which shareholders of independent firms agree to give up their stock in exchange for trust certificates that entitle them to a share of the trust's common profits. A group of trustees then operates the trust as a monopoly, controlling output and setting price.

Landmark Antitrust Legislation

- Congress began to formulate antitrust legislation in 1887, when it created the *Interstate Commerce Commission (ICC)* to oversee and correct abuses in the railroad industry.

Landmark Antitrust Legislation

- In 1890, Congress passed the *Sherman Act*, which declared every contract or conspiracy to restrain trade among states or nations illegal; and any attempt at monopoly, successful or not, a misdemeanor.

Landmark Antitrust Legislation

- The *rule of reason* is a criterion introduced by the Supreme Court in 1911 to determine whether a particular action was illegal ("unreasonable") or legal ("reasonable") within the terms of the Sherman Act.

Landmark Antitrust Legislation

- The *Clayton Act*, passed by Congress in 1914, strengthened the Sherman Act and clarified the rule of reason. The act outlawed specific monopolistic behaviors such as tying contracts, price discrimination, and unlimited mergers.

Landmark Antitrust Legislation

- The *Federal Trade Commission (FTC),* created by Congress in 1914, was established to investigate the structure and behavior of firms engaging in interstate commerce, to determine what constitutes unlawful "unfair" behavior , and to issue cease-and-desist orders to those found in violation of antitrust law.

Landmark Antitrust Legislation

- A *per se rule* is a rule enunciated by the courts declaring a particular action or outcome to be a per se (intrinsic) violation of antitrust law, whether the result is reasonable or not.

- For example, price fixing is illegal whether the resulting price is reasonable or not.

The Enforcement of Antitrust Law

- The *Antirust Division (of the Department of Justice)* is one of two federal agencies empowered to act against those in violation of antitrust laws. It initiates action against those who violate antitrust laws and decides which cases to prosecute and against whom to bring criminal charges.

Sanctions and Remedies

- The courts are empowered to impose a number of remedies if they find that antitrust law has been violated.

- *Consent decrees* are formal agreements on remedies between all the parties to an antitrust case that must be approved by the courts. Consent decrees can be signed before, during, or after a trial.

Sanctions and Remedies

- The penalties for violating antitrust laws have become more severe.

- *Treble damages* are awards to any person or private company that sustains injury or financial loss because of an antitrust violation, which are three times the actual damages.

Natural Monopoly

- A *natural monopoly* is an industry that realizes such large economies of scale in producing its product that single-firm production of that good or service is most efficient.

Natural Monopoly

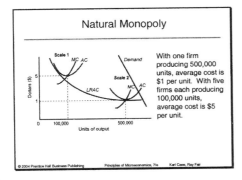

With one firm producing 500,000 units, average cost is $1 per unit. With five firms each producing 100,000 units, average cost is $5 per unit.

Review Terms and Concepts

Antitrust Division (of the Department of Justice)

barrier to entry

Clayton Act

collusion

consent decree

Federal Trade Commission (FTC)

government failure

government franchise

imperfectly competitive industry

Interstate Commerce Commission (ICC)

market power

natural monopoly

patent

price discrimination

perfect price discrimination

per se rule

public choice theory

pure monopoly

rent-seeking behavior

rule of reason

Sherman Act

trust

CHAPTER

13

Monopolistic Competition and Oligopoly

Prepared by: Fernando Quijano and Yvonn Quijano

Characteristics of Different Market Organizations

	Number of firms	Products differentiated or homogeneous	Price a decision variable	Free entry	Distinguished by	Examples
Perfect competition	Many	Homogeneous	No	Yes	Price competition only	Wheat farmer Textile firm
Monopoly	One	A single, unique product	Yes	No	Still constrained by market demand	Public utility Patented Drug
Monopolistic competition	Many	Differentiated	Yes, but limited	Yes	Price and quality competition	Restaurants Hand soap
Oligopoly	Few	Either	Yes	Limited	Strategic behavior	Automobiles Aluminum

- Not every industry fits neatly into one of these categories; however, this is a useful framework for thinking about industry structure and behavior.

Monopolistic Competition

- A **monopolistically competitive industry** has the following characteristics:
  - A large number of firms
  - No barriers to entry
  - Product differentiation

Monopolistic Competition

- *Monopolistic competition* is a common form of industry (market) structure in the United States, characterized by a large number of firms, none of which can influence market price by virtue of size alone. Some degree of market power is achieved by firms producing differentiated products. New firms can enter and established firms can exit such an industry with ease.

Monopolistic Competition

Percentage of Value of Shipments Accounted for by the Largest Firms in Selected Industries, 1992

INDUSTRY DESIGNATION	FOUR LARGEST FIRMS	EIGHT LARGEST FIRMS	TWENTY LARGEST FIRMS	NUMBER OF FIRMS
Travel trailers and campers	26	36	50	761
Dolls	31	51	66	239
Wood office furniture	34	42	55	639
Book printing	32	45	59	890
Curtains and draperies	26.5	36.3	50.1	2012
Fresh or frozen seafood	13.6	22.9	42.2	586
Women's dresses	14.2	23.7	39.4	747
Miscellaneous plastic products	5	8	14	7522

Source: U.S. Department of Commerce, Bureau of the Census, 1997 Census of Manufactures, Concentration Ratios in Manufacturing, Subject Series EC92M31S, June, 2001

Product Differentiation, Advertising, and Social Welfare

- **Product differentiation** is a strategy that firms use to achieve market power. Accomplished by producing products that have distinct positive identities in consumers' minds. This differentiation is often accomplished through advertising.

Product Differentiation, Advertising, and Social Welfare

Total Advertising Expenditures in 2001

	DOLLARS (BILLIONS)
Newspapers	89.5
Television	54.4
Direct mail	44.7
Internet	5.8
Yellow pages	13.6
Radio	17.9
Magazines	11.1
Total	231.3

Source: McCann Erickson, Inc., Reported in U.S. Bureau of the Census, Statistical Abstract of the United States, 2002, Table 1263.

Product Differentiation, Advertising, and Social Welfare

Magazine Advertising Revenues by Category, 2001

	DOLLARS (MILLIONS)
Automotive	$1,688
Technology	
Telecommunications	223
Computers and software	817
Home furnishings and supplies	1,196
Toiletries and cosmetics	1,401
Apparel and accessories	1,316
Financial, insurance and real estate	962
Food and food products	1,207
Drugs and remedies	1,217
Retail stores	692
Beer wine and liquor	307
Sporting goods	279

Source: Publishers Information Bureau, Statistical Abstract of the United States, 2002, pg. 772

The Case for Product Differentiation and Advertising

- The advocates of free and open competition believe that differentiated products and advertising give the market system its vitality and are the basis of its power.

- Product differentiation helps to ensure high quality and efficient production.

The Case for Product Differentiation and Advertising

- Advertising provides consumers with the valuable information on product availability, quality, and price that they need to make efficient choices in the marketplace.

The Case Against Product Differentiation and Advertising

- Critics of product differentiation and advertising argue that they amount to nothing more than waste and inefficiency.

- Enormous sums are spent to create minute, meaningless, and possibly nonexistent differences among products.

The Case Against Product Differentiation and Advertising

- Advertising raises the cost of products and frequently contains very little information. Often, it is merely an annoyance.

- People exist to satisfy the needs of the economy, not vice versa.

- Advertising can lead to unproductive warfare and may serve as a barrier to entry, thus reducing real competition.

© 2004 Prentice Hall Business Publishing   Principles of Microeconomics, 7/e   Karl Case, Ray Fair

_____

_____

_____

_____

_____

_____

_____

Price and Output Determination in Monopolistic Competition

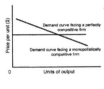

- The demand curve faced by a monopolistic competitor is likely to be *less elastic* than the demand curve faced by a perfectly competitive firm, but *more elastic* than the demand curve faced by a monopoly.

© 2004 Prentice Hall Business Publishing   Principles of Microeconomics, 7/e   Karl Case, Ray Fair

_____

_____

_____

_____

_____

_____

_____

Price/Output Determination in the Short Run

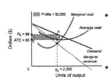

- In the short-run, a monopolistically competitive firm will produce up to the point where $MR = MC$.

- This firm is earning positive profits in the short-run.

© 2004 Prentice Hall Business Publishing   Principles of Microeconomics, 7/e   Karl Case, Ray Fair

_____

_____

_____

_____

_____

_____

_____

Price/Output
Determination in the Short Run

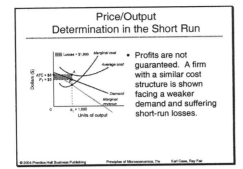

- Profits are not guaranteed. A firm with a similar cost structure is shown facing a weaker demand and suffering short-run losses.

Price/Output
Determination in the Long Run

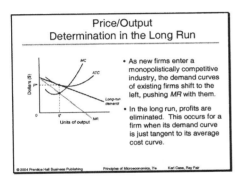

- As new firms enter a monopolistically competitive industry, the demand curves of existing firms shift to the left, pushing *MR* with them.

- In the long run, profits are eliminated. This occurs for a firm when its demand curve is just tangent to its average cost curve.

Economic Efficiency
and Resource Allocation

- In the long-run, economic profits are eliminated; thus, we might conclude that monopolistic competition is efficient, however:

  - Price is above marginal cost. More output could be produced at a resource cost below the value that consumers place on the product.

  - Average total cost is not minimized. The typical firm will not realize all the economies of scale available. Smaller and smaller market share results in excess capacity.

Oligopoly

- An *oligopoly* is a form of industry (market) structure characterized by a few dominant firms. Products may be homogeneous or differentiated.

Oligopoly

Percentage of Value of Shipments Accounted for by the Largest Firms in High-Concentration Industries, 1997

INDUSTRY DESIGNATION	FOUR LARGEST FIRMS	EIGHT LARGEST FIRMS	NUMBER OF FIRMS
Cellulosic man-made fiber	100	100	4
Primary copper	95	99	11
Household laundry equipment	90	99	10
Cigarettes	99	100	9
Malt beverages (beer)	90	95	494
Electric lamp bulbs	89	94	54
Cereal breakfast foods	83	94	48
Motor vehicles	83	92	325
Small arms ammunition	89	94	107
Household refrigerators and freezers	82	97	21

Source: U.S. Department of Commerce, Bureau of the Census, 1997 Census of Manufacturers, Concentration Ratios in Manufacturing, Subject Series 2001.

Oligopoly Models

- All kinds of oligopoly have one thing in common:

  - The behavior of any given oligopolistic firm depends on the behavior of the other firms in the industry.

The Collusion Model

- A group of firms that gets together and makes price and output decisions to maximize joint profits is called a *cartel*.

The Collusion Model

- Collusion occurs when price- and quantity-fixing agreements are explicit.

- *Tacit collusion* occurs when firms end up fixing price without a specific agreement, or when such agreements are implicit.

The Cournot Model

- The *Cournot model* is a model of a two-firm industry (duopoly) in which a series of output-adjustment decisions leads to a final level of output between the output that would prevail if the market were organized competitively and the output that would be set by a monopoly.

The Kinked Demand Curve Model

- The **kinked demand curve model** is a model of oligopoly in which the demand curve facing each individual firm has a "kink" in it. The kink follows from the assumption that competitive firms will follow if a single firm cuts price but will not follow if a single firm raises price.

The Kinked Demand Curve Model

- Above P*, an increase in price, which is not followed by competitors, results in a large decrease in the firm's quantity demanded (demand is elastic).

- Below P*, price decreases are followed by competitors so the firm does not gain as much quantity demanded (demand is inelastic).

The Price-Leadership Model

- **Price leadership** is a form of oligopoly in which one dominant firm sets prices and all the smaller firms in the industry follow its pricing policy.

The Price-Leadership Model

- The price-leadership model outcome:
  - The quantity demanded in the industry is split between the dominant firm and the group of smaller firms.
  - This division of output is determined by the amount of market power of the dominant firm.
  - The dominant firm has an incentive to push smaller firms out of the industry in order to establish a monopoly.

© 2004 Prentice Hall Business Publishing   Principles of Microeconomics, 7/e   Karl Case, Ray Fair

Predatory Pricing

- The practice of a large, powerful firm driving smaller firms out of the market by temporarily selling at an artificially low price is called *predatory pricing.*
- Such behavior became illegal in the United States with the passage of antimonopoly legislation around the turn of the century.

© 2004 Prentice Hall Business Publishing   Principles of Microeconomics, 7/e   Karl Case, Ray Fair

Game Theory

- *Game theory* analyzes oligopolistic behavior as a complex series of strategic moves and reactive countermoves among rival firms.
- In game theory, firms are assumed to anticipate rival reactions.

© 2004 Prentice Hall Business Publishing   Principles of Microeconomics, 7/e   Karl Case, Ray Fair

Payoff Matrix for Advertising Game

A's Strategy	B's Strategy	
	Do not advertise	Advertise
Do not advertise	A's profit = $50,000 / B's profit = $50,000	A's loss = $25,000 / B's profit = $75,000
Advertise	A's profit = $75,000 / B's loss = $25,000	A's profit = $10,000 / B's profit = $10,000

- The strategy that firm A will actually choose depends on the information available about B's likely strategy.

Game Theory

- Regardless of what B does, it pays for A to advertise. This is the *dominant strategy*, or the strategy that is best no matter what the opposition does.

Game Theory

- The *Prisoners' Dilemma* is a game in which:
  - The players are prevented from cooperating with each other;
  - Each player in isolation has a dominant strategy;
  - The dominant strategy makes each player worse off than in the case in which they could cooperate.

The Prisoners' Dilemma

Ginger	Rocky	
	Do not confess	Confess
Do not confess	Ginger: 1 year / Rocky: 1 year	Ginger: 7 years / Rocky: free
Confess	Ginger: Free / Rocky: 7 years	Ginger: 5 years / Rocky: 5 years

- Ginger and Rocky have dominant strategies to confess even though they would be better off if they both kept their mouths shut.

© 2004 Prentice Hall Business Publishing   Principles of Microeconomics, 7/e   Karl Case, Ray Fair

Payoff Matrixes for Left/Right-Top/Bottom Strategies

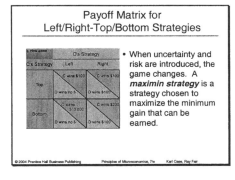

- In game theory, when all players are playing their best strategy given what their competitors are doing, the result is called *Nash equilibrium.*

© 2004 Prentice Hall Business Publishing   Principles of Microeconomics, 7/e   Karl Case, Ray Fair

Payoff Matrix for Left/Right-Top/Bottom Strategies

- When uncertainty and risk are introduced, the game changes. A *maximin strategy* is a strategy chosen to maximize the minimum gain that can be earned.

© 2004 Prentice Hall Business Publishing   Principles of Microeconomics, 7/e   Karl Case, Ray Fair

Repeated Games

- While explicit collusion violates the antitrust statutes, strategic reaction does not.
- Strategic reaction in a repeated game may still have the same effect as tacit collusion.

© 2004 Prentice Hall Business Publishing   Principles of Microeconomics, 7/e   Karl Case, Ray Fair

---

Repeated Games

- The strategy to respond in a way that lets your competitors know you will follow their lead is called *tit-for-tat strategy*. If one leads and the competitor follows, both will be better off.

© 2004 Prentice Hall Business Publishing   Principles of Microeconomics, 7/e   Karl Case, Ray Fair

---

Repeated Games

- Game theory has been used to help understand many phenomena – from the provision of local public goods and services to nuclear war.

© 2004 Prentice Hall Business Publishing   Principles of Microeconomics, 7/e   Karl Case, Ray Fair

Contestable Markets

- A market is *perfectly contestable* if entry to it *and* exit from it are costless.

- In contestable markets, even large oligopolistic firms end up behaving like perfectly competitive firms. Prices are pushed to long-run average cost by competition, and positive profits do not persist.

Contestable Markets

- The only necessary condition of oligopoly is that firms are large enough to have some control over price.

Contestable Markets

- Oligopolies are concentrated industries. At one extreme is the cartel, in essence, acting as a monopolist. At the other extreme, firms compete for small contestable markets in response to observed profits. In between are a number of alternative models, all of which stress the interdependence of oligopolistic firms.

Oligopoly and Economic Performance

- Oligopolies, or concentrated industries, are likely to be inefficient for the following reasons:
  - Profit-maximizing oligopolists are likely to price above marginal cost.
  - Strategic behavior can force firms into deadlocks that waste resources.
  - Product differentiation and advertising may pose a real danger of waste and inefficiency.

The Role of Government

- The *Celler-Kefauver Act of 1950* extended the government's authority to ban vertical and conglomerate mergers.

The Role of Government

- The *Herfindahl-Hirschman Index (HHI)* is a mathematical calculation that uses market share figures to determine whether or not a proposed merger will be challenged by the government.

Regulation of Mergers

Calculation of a Simple Herfindahl-Hirschman Index for Four Hypothetical Industries, Each With No More Than Four Firms

	PERCENTAGE SHARE OF:				HERFINDAHL-HIRSCHMAN INDEX
	FIRM 1	FIRM 2	FIRM 3	FIRM 4	
Industry A	50	50	–	–	$50^2 + 50^2 = 5,000$
Industry B	80	10	10	–	$80^2 + 10^2 + 10^2 = 6,600$
Industry C	25	25	25	25	$25^2 + 25^2 + 25^2 + 25^2 = 2,500$
Industry D	40	20	20	20	$40^2 + 20^2 + 20^2 + 20^2 = 2,800$

© 2004 Prentice Hall Business Publishing   Principles of Microeconomics, 7/e   Karl Case, Ray Fair

Department of Justice Merger Guidelines (revised 1984)

ANTITRUST DIVISION ACTION

HHI

Concentrated
Challenge if Index is raised by more than 50 points by the merger

1,800

Moderate Concentration
Challenge if Index is raised by more than 100 points by the merger

1,000

Unconcentrated
No challenge

0

© 2004 Prentice Hall Business Publishing   Principles of Microeconomics, 7/e   Karl Case, Ray Fair

Review Terms and Concepts

cartel
Collusion-Kefauver Act
Cournot model
dominant strategy
game theory
Herfindahl-Hirschman Index (HHI)
Kinked demand curve model
maximin strategy

monopolistic competition
Nash equilibrium
oligopoly
perfectly contestable market
price leadership
prisoners' dilemma
tit-for-tat strategy
product differentiation
tacit collusion

© 2004 Prentice Hall Business Publishing   Principles of Microeconomics, 7/e   Karl Case, Ray Fair

---

CHAPTER 14

Externalities, Public Goods,
Imperfect Information,
and Social Choice

Prepared by: Fernando Quijano
and Yvonn Quijano

© 2004 Prentice Hall Business Publishing   Principles of Microeconomics, 7/e   Karl Case, Ray Fair

---

Market Failure

- **Market failure** occurs when resources are misallocated or allocated inefficiently.

© 2004 Prentice Hall Business Publishing   Principles of Microeconomics, 7/e   Karl Case, Ray Fair

---

Externalities and Environmental Economics

- An **externality** is a cost or benefit resulting from some activity or transaction that is imposed or bestowed upon parties outside the activity or transaction. Sometimes called *spillovers* or *neighborhood effects*.

© 2004 Prentice Hall Business Publishing   Principles of Microeconomics, 7/e   Karl Case, Ray Fair

Marginal Social Cost and Marginal-Cost Pricing

- **Marginal social cost (MSC)** is the total cost to society of producing an additional unit of a good or service.

- *MSC* is equal to the sum of the marginal costs of producing the product and the correctly measured damage costs involved in the process of production.

© 2004 Prentice Hall Business Publishing   Principles of Microeconomics, 7/e   Karl Case, Ray Fair

Marginal Social Cost and Marginal-Cost Pricing

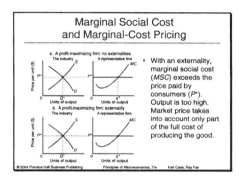

- With an externality, marginal social cost (*MSC*) exceeds the price paid by consumers (*P**). Output is too high. Market price takes into account only part of the full cost of producing the good.

© 2004 Prentice Hall Business Publishing   Principles of Microeconomics, 7/e   Karl Case, Ray Fair

Private Choices and External Effects

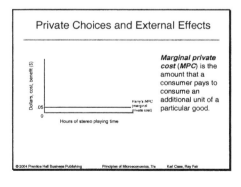

Marginal private cost (MPC) is the amount that a consumer pays to consume an additional unit of a particular good.

© 2004 Prentice Hall Business Publishing   Principles of Microeconomics, 7/e   Karl Case, Ray Fair

Private Choices and External Effects

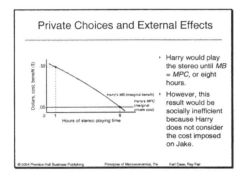

Marginal benefit (MB) is the benefit derived from each successive hour of music, or the maximum amount of money Harry is willing to pay for an additional hour of music.

© 2004 Prentice Hall Business Publishing   Principles of Microeconomics, 7/e   Karl Case, Ray Fair

---

Private Choices and External Effects

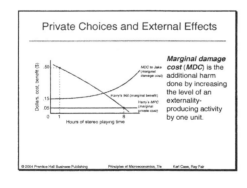

- Harry would play the stereo until MB = MPC, or eight hours.
- However, this result would be socially inefficient because Harry does not consider the cost imposed on Jake.

© 2004 Prentice Hall Business Publishing   Principles of Microeconomics, 7/e   Karl Case, Ray Fair

---

Private Choices and External Effects

Marginal damage cost (MDC) is the additional harm done by increasing the level of an externality-producing activity by one unit.

© 2004 Prentice Hall Business Publishing   Principles of Microeconomics, 7/e   Karl Case, Ray Fair

Private Choices and External Effects

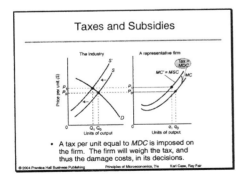

Marginal social cost (MSC) is the total cost to society of playing an additional hour of music.

- Playing the stereo beyond more than five hours is inefficient because the benefits to Harry are less than the social cost for every hour above five.

Internalizing Externalities

- Five approaches have been taken to solving the problem of externalities:

  1. government-imposed taxes and subsidies,
  2. private bargaining and negotiation,
  3. legal rules and procedures,
  4. sale or auctioning of rights to impose externalities, and
  5. direct government regulation.

Taxes and Subsidies

- A tax per unit equal to *MDC* is imposed on the firm. The firm will weigh the tax, and thus the damage costs, in its decisions.

Bargaining and Negotiation

- Government need not be involved in every case of externality.

- Private bargains and negotiations are likely to lead to an efficient solution in many social damage cases without any government involvement at all. This argument is referred to as the *Coase Theorem*.

Bargaining and Negotiation

- Three conditions must be satisfied for Coase's solution to work:
  - Basic rights at issue must be assigned and clearly understood.
  - There are no impediments to bargaining.
  - Only a few people can be involved.
- Bargaining will bring the contending parties to the right solution regardless of where rights are initially assigned.

Legal Rules and Procedures

- An *injunction* is a court order forbidding the continuation of behavior that leads to damages.

- *Liability rules* are laws that require A to compensate B for damages imposed.

Selling or Auctioning Pollution Rights

- The right to dump in a river or pollute the air or the ocean is a resource.

- Under the Clean Air Act of 1990, plants are issued tradable pollution rights. These rights can be sold at auction to those plants whose costs of compliance are highest.

Direct Regulation of Externalities

- Taxes, subsidies, legal rules, and public auction are all methods of *indirect* regulation designed to induce firms and households to weigh the social costs of their actions against the benefits.

Direct Regulation of Externalities

- *Direct* regulation includes legislation that regulates activities that, for example, are likely to harm the environment.

Public (Social) Goods

- **Public goods** (**social** or **collective goods**) are goods that are nonrival in consumption and/or their benefits are nonexcludable.

- Public goods have characteristics that make it difficult for the private sector to produce them profitably (market failure).

The Characteristics of Public Goods

- A good is **nonrival in consumption** when A's consumption of it does not interfere with B's consumption of it. The benefits of the good are collective—they accrue to everyone.

The Characteristics of Public Goods

- A good is **nonexcludable** if, once produced, no one can be excluded from enjoying its benefits. The good cannot be withheld from those that don't pay for it.

The Characteristics of Public Goods

- Because people can enjoy the benefits of public goods whether they pay for them or not, they are usually unwilling to pay for them. This is referred to as the *free-rider problem*.

© 2004 Prentice Hall Business Publishing   Principles of Microeconomics, 7/e   Karl Case, Ray Fair

The Characteristics of Public Goods

- The *drop-in-the-bucket problem* is another problem intrinsic to public goods: The good or service is usually so costly that its provision generally does not depend on whether or not any single person pays.

© 2004 Prentice Hall Business Publishing   Principles of Microeconomics, 7/e   Karl Case, Ray Fair

The Characteristics of Public Goods

- Consumers acting in their own self-interest have no incentive to contribute voluntarily to the production of public goods.
- Most people do not find room in their budgets for many voluntary payments. The economic incentive is missing.

© 2004 Prentice Hall Business Publishing   Principles of Microeconomics, 7/e   Karl Case, Ray Fair

Public Provision of Public Goods

- Public provision does not imply public production of public goods.

- Problems of public provision include frequent dissatisfaction. Individuals don't get to choose the quantity they want to buy—it is a collective purchase. We are all dissatisfied!

© 2004 Prentice Hall Business Publishing   Principles of Microeconomics, 7/e   Karl Case, Ray Fair

Optimal Provision of Public Goods

- With private goods, consumers decide what quantity to buy; market demand is the sum of those quantities at each price.

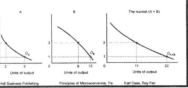

© 2004 Prentice Hall Business Publishing   Principles of Microeconomics, 7/e   Karl Case, Ray Fair

Optimal Provision of Public Goods

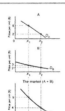

- With public goods, there is only one level of output, and consumers are willing to pay different amounts for each level.

- The market demand for a public good is the vertical sum of the amounts that individual households are willing to pay for each potential level of output.

© 2004 Prentice Hall Business Publishing   Principles of Microeconomics, 7/e   Karl Case, Ray Fair

Optimal Production of a Public Good

The *optimal level of provision for public goods* means producing as long as society's total willingness to pay per unit $D_{(A+B)}$ is greater than the marginal cost of producing the good.

Local Provision of Public Goods

- According to the *Tiebout hypothesis*, an efficient mix of public goods is produced when local land/housing prices and taxes come to reflect consumer preferences just as they do in the market for private goods.

Imperfect Information and Adverse Selection

- Most voluntary exchanges are efficient, but in the presence of imperfect information, not all exchanges are efficient.

- *Adverse selection* can occur when a buyer or seller enters into an exchange with another party who has more information.

Moral Hazard

- *Moral hazard* arises when one party to a contract passes the cost of his or her behavior on to the other party to the contract.

Moral Hazard

- The moral hazard problem is an information problem in which contracting parties cannot always determine the future behavior of the person with whom they are contracting.

Market Solutions

- As with any other good, there is an efficient quantity of information production.
- Like consumers, profit-maximizing firms will gather information as long as the marginal benefits from continued search are greater than the marginal costs.

Government Solutions

- Information is nonrival in consumption.
- When information is very costly for individuals to collect and disperse, it may be cheaper for government to produce it once for everybody.

Social Choice

- **Social choice** is the problem of deciding what society wants. The process of adding up individual preferences to make a choice for society as a whole.

The Impossibility Theorem

- The **impossibility theorem** is a proposition demonstrated by Kenneth Arrow showing that no system of aggregating individual preferences into social decisions will always yield consistent, nonarbitrary results.

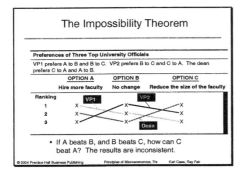

The Impossibility Theorem

Preferences of Three Top University Officials

VP1 prefers A to B and B to C. VP2 prefers B to C and C to A. The dean prefers C to A and A to B.

	OPTION A	OPTION B	OPTION C
	Hire more faculty	No change	Reduce the size of the faculty

Ranking
1 X (VP1) ... X (VP2) ... X
2 X ... X ... X
3 X ... X (Dean) ... X

- If A beats B, and B beats C, how can C beat A? The results are inconsistent.

© 2004 Prentice Hall Business Publishing   Principles of Microeconomics, 7/e   Karl Case, Ray Fair

The Voting Paradox

- The **voting paradox** is a simple demonstration of how majority-rule voting can lead to seemingly contradictory and inconsistent results. A commonly cited illustration of inconsistency described in the impossibility theorem.

Results of Voting on University's Plans: The Voting Paradox

	VOTES OF:			
Vote	VP1	VP2	Dean	Result [a]
A versus B	A	B	A	A wins: A > B
B versus C	B	B	C	B wins: B > C
C versus A	A	C	C	C wins: C > A

[a] A > B is read "A is preferred to B."

© 2004 Prentice Hall Business Publishing   Principles of Microeconomics, 7/e   Karl Case, Ray Fair

The Voting Paradox

- **Logrolling** occurs when congressional representatives trade votes, agreeing to help each other get certain pieces of legislation passed.

© 2004 Prentice Hall Business Publishing   Principles of Microeconomics, 7/e   Karl Case, Ray Fair

Government Inefficiency: Theory of Public Choice

- Government officials are assumed to maximize their own utility, not the social good.
- To understand the way government functions, we need to look less at the preferences of individual members of society and more at the incentive structures that exist around public officials.

© 2004 Prentice Hall Business Publishing   Principles of Microeconomics, 7/e   Karl Case, Ray Fair

Government Inefficiency: Theory of Public Choice

- Like voters, public officials suffer from a lack of incentive to become fully informed and to make tough choices.
- This is the viewpoint of what is called the *public choice* field in economics that builds heavily on the work of Nobel Laureate James Buchanan.

© 2004 Prentice Hall Business Publishing   Principles of Microeconomics, 7/e   Karl Case, Ray Fair

Rent Seeking Revisited

- There are reasons to believe that government attempts to produce the right goods and services in the right quantities efficiently may fail.
- The existence of an "optimal" level of public-goods production does not guarantee that governments will achieve it.

© 2004 Prentice Hall Business Publishing   Principles of Microeconomics, 7/e   Karl Case, Ray Fair

Government and the Market

- Governments can fail to produce an efficient allocation of resources for a number of reasons:

  1. Measurement of social damages and benefits is difficult and imprecise.

  2. There is no precise mechanism for determining citizens' preferences for public goods.

  3. Government agencies are not subject to the discipline of the market.

  4. It is naïve to expect elected and appointed officials to act selflessly for the good of society.

Review Terms and Concepts

adverse selection
Coase theorem
drop-in-the-bucket problem
externality
free-rider problem
impossibility theorem
injunction
liability rules

logrolling
marginal damage cost (MDC)
marginal private cost (MPC)
marginal social cost (MSC)
market failure
moral hazard
nonexcludable

nonrival in consumption
optimal level of provision for public goods
public goods (social or collective goods)
social choice
Tiebout hypothesis
voting paradox

CHAPTER 15

Income Distribution and Poverty

Prepared by: Fernando Quijano
and Yvonn Quijano

Income Distribution and Poverty

- This chapter focuses on distribution. Why do some people get more than others? What are the sources of inequality? Should the government change the distribution generated by the market?

- *Equity* means fairness.

The Utility Possibilities Frontier

- The *utility possibilities frontier* is a graphic representation of a two-person world that shows all points at which A's utility can be increased only if B's utility is decreased.

The Utility Possibilities Frontier

- Any point inside the utility possibilities frontier is inefficient. At point A, both I and J could be better off.

- Point B is preferable to point A.

- Both B and C are efficient, but may not be equally desirable.

The Sources of Household Income

- Households derive their incomes from three basic sources:
  - from wages or salaries received in exchange for labor,
  - from property—that is, capital, land, and so forth; and
  - from government.

Wages and Salaries

- All factors of production are paid a return equal to their marginal revenue product—the market value of what they produce at the margin.

- The rewards of a skill that is limited in supply depend on the demand for that skill. People with rare skills can make enormous salaries.

Wages and Salaries

- *Human capital* is the stock of knowledge, skills, and talents that people possess; it can be inborn or acquired through education and training.

Wages and Salaries

- **Compensating differentials** are differences in wages that result from differences in working conditions. Risky jobs usually pay higher wages; highly desirable jobs usually pay lower wages.

Wages and Salaries

- **Minimum wage** is the lowest wage that firms are permitted to pay workers.

- Another cause of inequality in the United States is *unemployment*.

- People earn wages only when they have jobs.

Effect of Minimum Wage Legislation

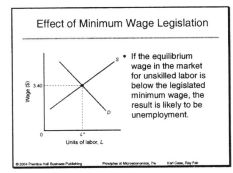

- If the equilibrium wage in the market for unskilled labor is below the legislated minimum wage, the result is likely to be unemployment.

Effect of Minimum Wage Legislation

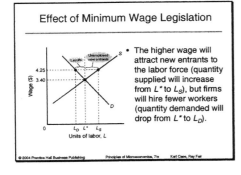

- The higher wage will attract new entrants to the labor force (quantity supplied will increase from L^* to L_S), but firms will hire fewer workers (quantity demanded will drop from L^* to L_D).

Income from Property

- **Property income** is income derived from the ownership of real property and financial holdings. It takes the form of profits, interest, dividends, and rents.

Income from Property

- The amount of property income that a household earns depends on:
  - how much property it owns, and
  - what kinds of assets it owns.

Income from Government

- *Transfer payments* are payments by the government to people who do not supply goods or services in exchange.
- Transfer programs are part of the government's attempts to offset some of the problems of inequality and poverty.

The Distribution of Income

- *Economic income* is the amount of money a household can spend during a given period without increasing or decreasing its net assets.
- Wages, salaries, dividends, interest income, transfer payments, rents, and so forth are sources of economic income.

Income Inequality in the United States

Distribution of Total Income and Components in the United States, 2000 (Percentages)

HOUSEHOLDS	TOTAL INCOME	WAGES AND SALARIES	PROPERTY INCOME	TRANSFER INCOME
Bottom fifth	2.7	1.7	0.7	19.2
Second fifth	7.2	6.3	4.2	25.8
Third fifth	12.6	12.7	9.2	23.0
Fourth fifth	21.3	23.6	15.1	17.0
Top fifth	56.7	55.6	73.2	14.8
Top 1 percent	14.8	10.4	31.6	1.2

Source: Julie-Anne Cronin, US Department of the Treasury, OTA Paper 85, pg 19.

Changes in the Distribution of Income

- ***Money income*** is a measure
  of income used by the Census
  Bureau. Because it excludes
  noncash transfer payments
  and capital gains income, it is
  less inclusive than "economic
  income."

Changes in the Distribution of Income

Distribution of Money Income of U.S. Families by Quintiles, 1947 – 2000 (Percentages)

	1947	1960	1972	1980	1984	1994	1997	2000
Bottom fifth	5.0	4.8	5.4	5.2	4.7	4.2	4.2	4.3
Second fifth	11.8	12.2	11.9	11.5	11.0	10.0	9.9	9.8
Third fifth	17.0	17.8	17.5	17.5	17.0	15.7	15.7	15.5
Fourth fifth	23.1	24.0	23.9	24.3	24.4	23.3	23.0	22.8
Top fifth	43.0	41.3	41.4	41.5	42.9	46.9	47.2	47.4
Top 5 percent	17.2	15.9	15.9	15.3	16.0	20.1	20.7	20.8

Source: Statistical Abstract of the United States, various editions; Department of Commerce, HHES Division.

The Lorenz Curve
and the Gini Coefficient

- The ***Lorenz curve*** is a widely
  used graph of the distribution
  of income, with cumulative
  percentage of families plotted
  along the horizontal axis and
  cumulative percentage of
  income plotted along the
  vertical axis.

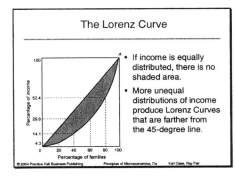

The Lorenz Curve

- If income is equally distributed, there is no shaded area.
- More unequal distributions of income produce Lorenz Curves that are farther from the 45-degree line.

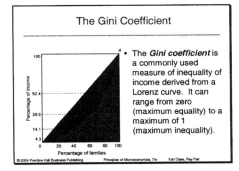

The Gini Coefficient

- The *Gini coefficient* is a commonly used measure of inequality of income derived from a Lorenz curve. It can range from zero (maximum equality) to a maximum of 1 (maximum inequality).

Differences Between
African-American Households, White
Households, and Single-Person Households

Distribution of Money Income of Households, 2000 (Percentages)

	ALL HOUSEHOLDS	AFRICAN-AMERICAN HOUSEHOLDS	WHITE HOUSEHOLDS	HISPANIC HOUSEHOLDS	ONE-PERSON HOUSEHOLDS
0-15,000	16.0	26.0	14.8	18.8	36.3
15-25,000	13.4	16.5	13.0	18.3	19.9
25-35,000	12.5	12.9	12.6	14.7	14.4
35-50,000	15.5	16.8	15.4	17.7	13.1
50-75,000	18.9	15.2	19.4	17.4	9.7
75,-100,000	10.4	6.5	11.0	7.4	3.5
>100,000	13.4	6.1	14.2	5.8	3.1
Total	100.0	100.0	100.0	100.0	100.0

Note: Totals may not add to 100 due to rounding.
Source: Statistical Abstract of the United States, 2002, Tables 659 and 664.

© 2004 Prentice Hall Business Publishing   Principles of Microeconomics, 7/e   Karl Case, Ray Fair

Poverty

- In simplest terms, poverty is the condition of people who have very low incomes.

- The *poverty line* is the officially established income level that distinguishes the poor form the nonpoor. It is set at three times the cost of the Department of Agriculture's minimum food budget.

Poverty in the United States Since 1960

Percentage of Persons in Poverty by Demographic Group, 1964 - 2001

	OFFICIAL MEASURE 1964	OFFICIAL MEASURE 2001
All	19.0	11.7
White	14.9	9.9
African-American	49.6	22.7
Hispanic	NA	21.4
Female householder – no husband present	45.9	26.4
Elderly (65+)	28.5	10.1
Children under 18	20.7	16.3

Includes food, housing, and medical benefits.
Source: Statistical Abstract of the United States, 2002.

The Distribution of Wealth

- The distribution of wealth is much more unequal than the distribution of income. Wealth is passed from generation to generation and accumulates.

- Some argue that unequal distribution of wealth is a natural consequence of risk taking in a market economy.

The Distribution of Wealth

Percentage of Different Assets Owned by Households, 1998 *Survey of Consumer Finances*

PERCENTAGE OF OWNERS	COMMON STOCK EXCLUDING PENSIONS	ALL COMMON STOCK	NONEQUITY FINANCIAL ASSETS	HOUSING EQUITY	NET WORTH
Top .5 percent	41.4	37.0	24.2	10.2	25.6
Top 1 percent	53.2	47.7	32.0	14.8	34.0
Top 10 percent	91.2	86.2	72.2	50.7	68.9
Bottom 80 percent	1.7	4.1	14.0	29.3	18.5

Source: James Poterba, "Stock Market Wealth and Consumption," Journal of Economic Perspectives, 14(2), 99 – 118 , Spring 2000.

© 2004 Prentice Hall Business Publishing   Principles of Microeconomics, 7/e   Karl Case, Ray Fair

The Redistribution Debate

- Philosophical arguments against redistribution:
  - The market, when left to operate on its own, is fair. "One is entitled to the fruits of one's efforts."
  - Taxation of income for redistribution purposes is against "freedom of contract" and the protection of property rights.

© 2004 Prentice Hall Business Publishing   Principles of Microeconomics, 7/e   Karl Case, Ray Fair

The Redistribution Debate

- Arguments against redistribution:
  - Taxation and transfer programs interfere with the incentives to work, save, and invest.
  - Bureaucratic waste and inefficiency is inevitable in the administration of social programs.

© 2004 Prentice Hall Business Publishing   Principles of Microeconomics, 7/e   Karl Case, Ray Fair

The Redistribution Debate

- Arguments in favor of redistribution:
  - A wealthy country, such as the United States, has the moral obligation to provide all its members with the necessities of life. The Constitution does carry a guarantee of the "right to life."

The Redistribution Debate

- Arguments in favor of redistribution:
  - *Utilitarian justice* is the idea that "a dollar in the hand of a rich person is worth less than a dollar in the hand of a poor person." If the marginal utility of income declines with income, transferring income from the rich to the poor will increase total utility.

The Redistribution Debate

- Arguments in favor of redistribution:
  - *Rawlsian justice* is a theory of distributional justice that concludes that the social contract emerging from the "original position" would call for an income distribution that would maximize the well-being of the worst-off member of society.

The Works of Karl Marx

- Marx did not write very much about socialism or communism.

- He wrote a critique of capitalism, but was not very clear about what would replace it.

- In one essay he wrote, "from each according to his ability, to each according to his needs."

The Works of Karl Marx

- The *labor theory of value*, stated most simply, is the theory that the value of a commodity depends only on the amount of labor required to produce it.

- The owners of capital are able to extract "surplus value" out of labor.

Redistribution Programs and Policies

- The income tax is *progressive*— those with higher incomes pay a higher percentage of their incomes in taxes.

- The individual income tax is only one tax among many.

Redistribution Programs and Policies

- Most studies of the effect of taxes on the distribution of income have concluded that the overall burden is roughly proportional. In other words:
  - All people pay about the same percentage of their income in total taxes.

Redistribution Programs and Policies

Effective Rates of Federal, State, and Local Taxes, 2000
(Taxes as a Percentage of Total Income)

	FEDERAL	TOTAL
Bottom 20%	5.9	28.1
Second 20	11.7	26.3
Third 20	17.4	29.2
Fourth 20	20.1	32.6
Top 20	24.6	33.9
Top 10	25.7	34.5
Top 5	26.6	34.9
Top 1	29.1	37.0

Source: Julie-Anne Cronin, US Department of the Treasury, OTA Paper 85 and authors' estimate.

Expenditure Programs

- The *Social Security system* is a federal system of social insurance programs. It includes three separate programs that are financed through separate trust funds:
  - the Old Age and Survivors Insurance (OASI) program,
  - the Disability Insurance (DI) program, and
  - the Health Insurance (HI, or Medicare) program.

Expenditure Programs

- **Public assistance**, or **welfare**, consists of government transfer programs that provide cash benefits to:

  1. families with dependent children whose incomes and assets fall below a very low level, and

  2. the very poor, regardless of whether or not they have children.

Expenditure Programs

- The *Supplemental Security Income (SSI)* program is designed to take care of the elderly who end up very poor and have no, or very low Social Security entitlement.

Expenditure Programs

- **Unemployment compensation** is a state government transfer program that pays cash benefits for a certain period of time to laid-off workers who have worked for a specified period of time for a covered employer.

Expenditure Programs

- *Medicaid* and *Medicare* are in-kind government transfer programs that provide health and hospitalization benefits:
  - Medicare to the aged and their survivors and to certain of the disabled, regardless of income, and Medicaid to people with low incomes.

Expenditure Programs

- *Food stamps* are vouchers that have a face value greater than their cost and that can be used to purchase food at grocery stores.

Expenditure Programs

- Housing programs are designed to improve the quality of life for low-income people.
- The Earned Income Tax Credit is an important program that allows lower income families with children a credit equal to a percentage of all wage and salary income against their income taxes.

Review Terms and Concepts

compensating differentials   money income

economic income   poverty line

equity   property income

food stamps   public assistance, or welfare

Gini coefficient   Rawlsian justice

human capital   Social Security system

labor theory of value   transfer payments

Lorenz curve   unemployment compensation

Medicaid and Medicare   utilitarian justice

minimum wage   utility possibilities frontier

CHAPTER 16

Public Finance:
The Economics of Taxation

Prepared by: Fernando Quijano
and Yvonn Quijano

The Economics of Taxation

- The primary vehicle that the government uses to finance itself is taxation.

- Taxes may be imposed on transactions, institutions, property, meals, and other things, but in the final analysis they are paid by individuals or households.

Taxes: Basic Concepts

- The *tax base* is the measure or value upon which a tax is levied.

- The *tax rate structure* is the percentage of a tax base that must be paid in taxes—25% of income, for example.

© 2004 Prentice Hall Business Publishing   Principles of Microeconomics, 7/e   Karl Case, Ray Fair

---

Taxes on Economic "Flows"

- Most taxes are levied on measurable economic flows.

- For example, a profits, or net income, tax is levied on the annual profits earned by corporations.

© 2004 Prentice Hall Business Publishing   Principles of Microeconomics, 7/e   Karl Case, Ray Fair

---

Taxes on Stocks versus Taxes on Flows

Federal Government Receipts 1960-2003 (billions of dollars)

	Individual Income Tax	Corporation Income Tax	Social Insur. Payroll Taxes	Excise Taxes	Other Receipts	Total
1960	40.7	21.5	14.7	11.7	3.9	92.5
%	44.0	23.2	15.9	12.6	4.2	100
1970	90.4	32.8	44.4	15.7	9.5	192.8
%	46.9	17.0	23.0	8.1	4.9	100
1980	244.1	64.6	157.8	24.3	26.3	517.1
%	47.2	12.5	30.1	4.7	5.1	100
1990	466.9	93.5	380.0	35.3	56.2	1,032.0
%	45.2	9.1	36.8	3.4	5.4	100
2003*	849.1	143.2	726.6	68.4	49.0	1,836.2
%	46.3	7.8	40.0	3.7	2.7	100

* OMB estimate
Source: United States, Office of Management and Budget. Percentages may not add to 100 due to rounding.

© 2004 Prentice Hall Business Publishing   Principles of Microeconomics, 7/e   Karl Case, Ray Fair

Proportional, Progressive, and Regressive Taxes

- A *proportional tax* is a tax whose burden is the same proportion of income for all households.

© 2004 Prentice Hall Business Publishing   Principles of Microeconomics, 7/e   Karl Case, Ray Fair

---

Proportional, Progressive, and Regressive Taxes

- A *progressive tax* is a tax whose burden, expressed as a percentage of income, increases as income increases.

© 2004 Prentice Hall Business Publishing   Principles of Microeconomics, 7/e   Karl Case, Ray Fair

---

Proportional, Progressive, and Regressive Taxes

- A *regressive tax* is a tax whose burden, expressed as a percentage of income, falls as income increases.
- *Excise taxes* (taxes on specific commodities) are regressive. The retail sales tax is also regressive.

© 2004 Prentice Hall Business Publishing   Principles of Microeconomics, 7/e   Karl Case, Ray Fair

Proportional, Progressive, and Regressive Taxes

The Burden of a Hypothetical 5% Sales Tax Imposed on Three Households with Different Incomes

HOUSEHOLD	INCOME	SAVING RATE, %	SAVING	CONSUMPTION	5% TAX ON CONSUMPTION	TAX AS A % OF INCOME
A	$ 10,000	20	$ 2,000	$ 8,000	$ 400	4.0
B	20,000	40	8,000	12,000	600	3.0
C	50,000	50	25,000	25,000	1,250	2.5

Marginal versus Average Tax Rates

- The *average tax rate* is the total amount of tax you pay divided by your total income.

- The *marginal tax rate* is the tax rate you pay on any additional income you earn.

Marginal versus Average Tax Rates

Individual Income Tax Rates, 2003 MARRIED FILING JOINTLY		Individual Income Tax Rates, 2003 SINGLE	
TAXABLE INCOME	TAX RATE	TAXABLE INCOME	TAX RATE
$0 - 14,000	10%	$0 – 7,000	10%
$14,001 – 56,800	15%	$7,001 – 28,400	15%
$56,801 – 114,650	25%	$28,401 – 68,800	25%
$114,651 – 174,700	28%	$68,801 – 143,500	28%
$174,701 – 311,950	33%	$143,501 – 311,950	33%
More than $311,950	35%	More than $311,950	35%

Marginal versus Average Tax Rates

Tax Calculations for a Single Taxpayer Who Earned $80,000 in 2003	
Total income	$80,000
– Personal exemption	$3,050
– Standard deduction	$4,750
= Taxable income	$72,200
Tax Calculation	
0 - $7,000 taxed at 10% > $7,000 X .10 =	$700.00
$7,000 - $28,000 taxed at 15% > ($28,400 – $7,000) X .15 = $21,400 X .15 =	$3,210.00
$28,400 - $88,800 taxed at 25% > ($88,800 – 28,400) X .25 = $40,000 X .25 =	$10,100.00
income above $88,800 taxed at 28% > ($72,200 - $88,800) X .28 = $3,400 X .28 =	$952.00
Total tax =	$14,962.00
Average tax rate =	18.7%
Marginal tax rate =	28.0%

Marginal versus Average Tax Rates

- All taxpayers can subtract the *personal exemption* ($3,050 in 2003), and the *standard deduction* ($4,750 in 2003).

- Income is taxed in slices according to the income tax rates established by the government.

Marginal versus Average Tax Rates

- Marginal tax rates influence behavior. Decisions about how much to work and how much to invest depends in part on the after-tax return.

Tax Equity

- One theory of fairness is called the **benefits-received principle**, which holds that taxpayers should contribute to government (in the form of taxes) in proportion to the benefits that they receive from public expenditures.

Tax Equity

- Another theory of fairness is called the **ability-to-pay principle**, which holds that citizens should bear tax burdens in line with their ability to pay taxes.

- Two principles follow: *horizontal equity* and *vertical equity*.

Horizontal and Vertical Equity

- *Horizontal equity* holds that those with equal ability to pay should bear equal tax burdens.

- *Vertical equity* holds that those with greater ability to pay should pay more.

What is the "Best" Tax Base?

- The three leading candidates for best tax base are:
  - Income,
  - Consumption, and
  - Wealth

What is the "Best" Tax Base?

- Income—to be precise, *economic income*—is anything that enhances your ability to command resources.

Economic Income = Consumption + Change in Net Worth

- In economic terms, income is income, regardless of source and use.

What is the "Best" Tax Base?

- Consumption is the total value of things that a household consumes in a given period.

- Wealth, or net worth, is the value of all the things you own after your liabilities are subtracted.

Net Worth = Assets − Liabilities

Consumption as the Best Tax Base

- If we want to redistribute well-being, the tax base should be consumption because consumption is the best measure of well-being.

Consumption as the Best Tax Base

- Supporters of consumption as the tax base argue that a tax on income discourages saving by taxing savings twice. It also distorts the choice between consumption and saving.

- Double taxing also reduces the saving rate and the rate of investment—and ultimately the rate of economic growth.

Income as the Best Tax Base

- Supporters of the use of income as the tax base argue that your ability to pay is your ability to command resources.

- It is your income that enables you to save or consume, and it is income that should be taxed regardless of its sources and uses.

Wealth as the Best Tax Base

- Supporters of the use of wealth as the tax base argue that the real power to command resources comes not from income but from accumulated wealth.

The Gift and Estate Tax

- A person's *estate* is the property that a person owns at his or her death.

- An *estate tax* is a tax on the total value of a person's estate regardless of how it is distributed.

Tax Incidence: Who Pays?

- *Tax incidence* refers to the ultimate distribution of a tax's burden.

- *Sources side/uses side*: The impact of a tax may be felt on one or the other or on both sides of the income equation. Either income falls or the prices of goods and services rise.

Tax Incidence: Who Pays?

- **Tax shifting** occurs when households can alter their behavior and do something to avoid paying the tax.

- Final price changes in input and output markets determine the ultimate burden of the tax.

Tax Incidence: Who Pays?

- A tax such as the retail sales tax, which is levied at the same rate on all consumer goods, is harder to avoid, and therefore to be shifted.

- Broad-based taxes are less likely to be shifted and more likely to "stick" where they are levied than "partial taxes" are.

The Incidence of Payroll Taxes

- In 2003, 40 percent of federal revenues came from social security taxes, also called "payroll taxes."

- The payroll tax may lead firms to substitute capital for labor, and perhaps to cut production due to higher labor costs.

The Incidence of Payroll Taxes

- If the payroll tax reduces the demand for labor, wages will decrease, and part of the tax is thus passed on to the workers.

© 2004 Prentice Hall Business Publishing   Principles of Microeconomics, 7/e   Karl Case, Ray Fair

---

Labor Supply and Labor Demand Curves in Perfect Competition

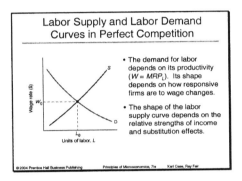

- The demand for labor depends on its productivity ($W = MRP_L$). Its shape depends on how responsive firms are to wage changes.

- The shape of the labor supply curve depends on the relative strengths of income and substitution effects.

© 2004 Prentice Hall Business Publishing   Principles of Microeconomics, 7/e   Karl Case, Ray Fair

---

Imposing a Payroll Tax: Who Pays?

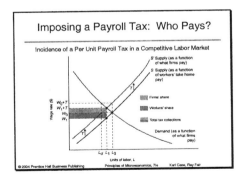

© 2004 Prentice Hall Business Publishing   Principles of Microeconomics, 7/e   Karl Case, Ray Fair

Imposing a Payroll Tax: Who Pays?

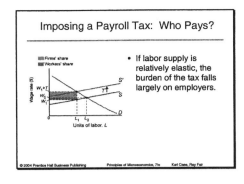

- If labor supply is relatively elastic, the burden of the tax falls largely on employers.

Imposing a Payroll Tax: Who Pays?

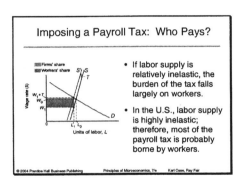

- If labor supply is relatively inelastic, the burden of the tax falls largely on workers.
- In the U.S., labor supply is highly inelastic; therefore, most of the payroll tax is probably borne by workers.

Imposing a Payroll Tax: Who Pays?

Estimated Incidence of Payroll Taxes in the United States in 2003

POPULATION RANKED BY INCOME	TAX AS A % OF TOTAL INCOME
Bottom 20%	7.6
Second 20%	9.8
Third 20%	10.7
Fourth 20%	11.2
Top 20%	8.0
Top 10%	6.7
Top 5%	5.3
Top 1%	3.0

The Incidence of Corporate Profits Taxes

- *Corporations* are firms granted limited liability status by the government.

- *Partnerships* and **proprietorships** do not enjoy limited liability and do not pay this tax; rather, they report their firms' income directly on their individual income tax returns.

The Incidence of Corporate Profits Taxes

- We can think of the corporate tax as a tax on *capital income*.

- If the corporate sector becomes less profitable as a result of the tax, capital investment begins to favor the nontaxed sector. The taxed sector contracts, and the nontaxed sector expands.

The Incidence of Corporate Profits Taxes

- As capital flows to the to nontaxed sector, competition springs up and prices are driven down.

- Some of the tax shifts to capital income earners in the noncorporate sector.

- Eventually, the after-tax profit rates in the two sectors are equal.

The Incidence of Corporate Profits Taxes

- Taxed firms will have an incentive to substitute labor for capital. This could benefit labor by driving up wages.

- Owners of corporations, proprietorships, and partnerships all bear the burden of the corporate tax in rough proportion to profits, even though it is directly levied only on corporations.

The Burden of the Corporate Tax

- The ultimate burden of the corporate tax depends on:

  1. The relative capital/labor intensity of the two sectors.

  2. The ease with which capital and labor can be substituted in the two sectors.

  3. The elasticities of demand for the products of each sector.

The Burden of the Corporate Tax

Estimated Burden of the U.S. Corporation Income Tax in 2003

POPULATION RANKED BY INCOME	TAX AS A % OF TOTAL INCOME
Bottom 20%	0.5
Second 20%	1.0
Third 20%	1.4
Fourth 20%	1.5
Top 20%	4.6
Top 10%	5.8
Top 5%	7.2
Top 1%	9.7

The Overall Incidence of Taxes in the United States: Empirical Evidence

- State and local taxes (with sales taxes playing a big role) seem as a group to be mildly regressive.

- Federal taxes, dominated by the individual income tax but increasingly affected by the regressive payroll tax, are mildly progressive.

- The overall system is mildly progressive.

Excess Burdens and the Principle of Neutrality

- The *total burden* of a tax is the sum of the revenue collected form the tax and the excess burden created by the tax.

- An ***excess burden*** is the amount by which the burden of a tax exceeds the total revenue collected. Also called the *dead weight loss*.

Excess Burdens and the Principle of Neutrality

- The ***principle of neutrality*** states that, all else equal, taxes that are neutral with respect to economic decisions are generally preferable to taxes that distort economic decisions.

- Taxes that are not neutral impose excess burdens.

How Do Excess Burdens Arise?

Technology	Input requirements per unit of output X		Per unit cost of X $= K(P_K) + L(P_L)$
	K	L	$P_K = \$2$ $P_L = \$2$
A	7	3	$20 → Least cost
B	4	7	$22

- If the industry is competitive, long-run equilibrium price will be $20 per unit of X. If 1,000 units of X are sold, consumers will pay a total of $20,000 for X.

© 2004 Prentice Hall Business Publishing　　　Principles of Microeconomics, 7/e　　　Karl Case, Ray Fair

How Do Excess Burdens Arise?

Technology	Input requirements per unit of output X		Per unit cost of X $= K(P_K) + L(P_L)$
	K	L	$P_K = \$2 + \$1\,tax = \$3$ $P_L = \$2$
A	7	3	$27 → Least cost
B	4	7	$26

- If the industry is competitive, price will be $26 per unit of X when a tax of $1 per unit of capital is imposed. If technology B is used, and sales remain at 1,000 units, total tax collections will be $4,000, but consumers will pay $26,000, or $6,000 more than before the tax.

© 2004 Prentice Hall Business Publishing　　　Principles of Microeconomics, 7/e　　　Karl Case, Ray Fair

How Do Excess Burdens Arise?

- The larger the distortion that a tax causes in behavior, the larger the excess burden of the tax. Taxes levied on broad bases tend to distort choices less and impose smaller excess burdens than taxes on more sharply defined bases.

© 2004 Prentice Hall Business Publishing　　　Principles of Microeconomics, 7/e　　　Karl Case, Ray Fair

The Principle of Second Best

- A distorting tax is sometimes desirable when other distortions already exist in the economy. This is called the *principle of second best*.

- A distorting tax can improve economic welfare when there are other taxes present that already distort economic decisions.

Measuring Excess Burdens

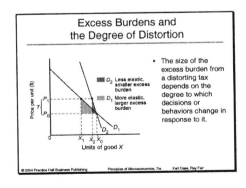

- A tax that alters economic decisions imposes a burden that exceeds the amount of taxes collected.

- An excise tax that raises the price of a good above marginal cost drives some consumers to buy less-desirable substitutes, reducing consumer surplus.

Excess Burdens and the Degree of Distortion

- The size of the excess burden from a distorting tax depends on the degree to which decisions or behaviors change in response to it.

Excess Burdens and the Degree of Distortion

- If demand were perfectly inelastic, no distortion would occur.

- Because land is in perfectly inelastic supply, a uniform tax on all land uses distorts economic decisions less than taxes levied on other factors of production that are in variable supply.

© 2004 Prentice Hall Business Publishing   Principles of Microeconomics, 7/e   Karl Case, Ray Fair

Review Terms and Concepts

ability-to-pay principle	principle of second best
average tax rate	progressive tax
benefits-received principle	proportional tax
corporation	proprietorship
estate	regressive tax
estate tax	sources side/uses side
excess burden	tax base
marginal tax rate	tax incidence
partnership	tax rate structure
principle of neutrality	tax shifting

© 2004 Prentice Hall Business Publishing   Principles of Microeconomics, 7/e   Karl Case, Ray Fair

CHAPTER 17

International Trade, Comparative Advantage, and Protectionism

Prepared by: Fernando Quijano and Yvonn Quijano

© 2004 Prentice Hall Business Publishing   Principles of Microeconomics, 7/e   Karl Case, Ray Fair

Trade Surpluses and Deficits

U.S. Balance of Trade (Exports Minus Imports), 1929–2002 (Billions of Dollars)

	EXPORTS MINUS IMPORTS		EXPORTS MINUS IMPORTS
1929	+ 0.4	1986	– 131.9
1933	+ 0.1	1987	– 142.3
1945	– 0.9	1988	– 106.3
1955	+ 0.4	1989	– 80.7
1960	+ 2.4	1990	– 71.4
1965	+ 3.9	1991	– 20.7
1970	+ 1.2	1992	– 27.9
1975	+ 13.6	1993	– 60.5
1976	– 2.3	1994	– 87.1
1977	– 23.7	1995	– 84.3
1978	– 26.1	1996	– 89.0
1979	– 24.0	1997	– 89.3
1980	– 14.9	1998	– 151.7
1981	– 15.0	1999	– 249.9
1982	– 20.5	2000	– 365.5
1983	– 51.7	2001	– 348.9
1984	– 102.0	2002	– 423.6
1985	– 114.2		

Source: U.S. Department of Commerce, Bureau of Economic Analysis

The Economic Basis for Trade: Comparative Advantage

- *Corn Laws* were the tariffs, subsidies, and restrictions enacted by the British Parliament in the early nineteenth century to discourage imports and encourage exports of grain.

The Economic Basis for Trade: Comparative Advantage

- David Ricardo's *theory of comparative advantage*, which he used to argue against the corn laws, states that specialization and free trade will benefit all trading partners (real wages will rise), even those that may be absolutely less efficient producers.

Absolute Advantage versus Comparative Advantage

- A country enjoys an **absolute advantage** over another country in the production of a product when it uses fewer resources to produce that product than the other country does.

© 2004 Prentice Hall Business Publishing   Principles of Microeconomics, 7/e   Karl Case, Ray Fair

---

Absolute Advantage versus Comparative Advantage

- A country enjoys a **comparative advantage** in the production of a good when that good can be produced at a lower cost *in terms of other goods*.

© 2004 Prentice Hall Business Publishing   Principles of Microeconomics, 7/e   Karl Case, Ray Fair

---

Gains from Mutual Absolute Advantage

Yield Per Acre Of Wheat And Cotton

	NEW ZEALAND	AUSTRALIA
Wheat	6 bushels	2 bushels
Cotton	2 bales	6 bales

- New Zealand can produce three times the wheat that Australia can on one acre of land, and Australia can produce three times the cotton.
- We say that the two countries have *mutual absolute advantage*.

© 2004 Prentice Hall Business Publishing   Principles of Microeconomics, 7/e   Karl Case, Ray Fair

Gains from Mutual Absolute Advantage

- Suppose that each country divides its land to obtain equal units of cotton and wheat production as shown below:

Total Production Of Wheat And Cotton Assuming No Trade, Mutual Absolute Advantage, And 100 Available Acres

	NEW ZEALAND	AUSTRALIA
Wheat	25 acres x 6 bushels/acre 150 bushels	75 acres x 2 bushels/acre 150 bushels
Cotton	75 acres x 2 bales/acre 150 bales	25 acres x 6 bales/acre 150 bales

Production Possibility Frontiers for Australia and New Zealand Before Trade

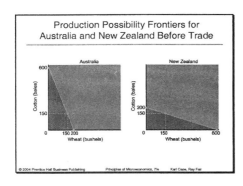

Gains from Mutual Absolute Advantage

- An agreement to trade 300 bushels of wheat for 300 bales of cotton would double both wheat and cotton consumption in both countries.

Production and Consumption of Wheat and Cotton after Specialization

	PRODUCTION		CONSUMPTION	
	New Zealand	Australia	New Zealand	Australia
Wheat	100 acres x 6 bu/acre 600 bushels	0 acres 0	300 bushels	300 bushels
Cotton	0 acres 0	100 acres x 6 bales/acre 600 bales	300 bales	300 bales

Expanded Possibilities after Trade

- Because both countries have an absolute advantage in the production of one product, specialization and trade will benefit both.

Gains from Comparative Advantage

- Even if a country had a considerable absolute advantage in the production of both goods, Ricardo would argue that *specialization and trade are still mutually beneficial.*

Gains from Comparative Advantage

- When countries specialize in producing the goods in which they have a comparative advantage, they maximize their combined output and allocate their resources more efficiently.

Gains from Comparative Advantage

- Assume that people in each country want to consume equal amounts of cotton and wheat, and that each country is constrained by its domestic production possibilities curve, as follows:

Yield Per Acre of Wheat and Cotton

	NEW ZEALAND	AUSTRALIA
Wheat	6 bushels	1 bushel
Cotton	6 bales	3 bales

Gains from Comparative Advantage

Total Production of Wheat and Cotton Assuming No Trade and 100 Available Acres

	NEW ZEALAND	AUSTRALIA
Wheat	50 acres x 6 bushels/acre 300 bushels	75 acres x 1 bushels/acre 75 bushels
Cotton	50 acres x 6 bales/acre 300 bales	25 acres x 3 bales/acre 75 bales

- The gains from trade in this example can be demonstrated in three stages.

Realizing a Gain from Trade When One Country Has a Double Absolute Advantage

Stage 1: Countries specialize

	STAGE 1	
	New Zealand	Australia
Wheat	50 acres x 6 bushels/acre 300 bushels	0 acres 0
Cotton	50 acres x 6 bales/acre 300 bales	100 acres x 3 bales/acre 300 bales

- Australia transfers all its land into cotton production. New Zealand cannot completely specialize in wheat production because it needs 300 bales of cotton and will not be able to get enough cotton from Australia (if countries are to consume equal amounts of cotton and wheat).

Realizing a Gain from Trade When One Country Has a Double Absolute Advantage

Stage 2:

STAGE 2		
	New Zealand	*Australia*
Wheat	75 acres x 6 bushels/acre 450 bushels	0 acres 0
Cotton	25 acres x 6 bales/acre 150 bales	100 acres x 3 bales/acre 300 bales

- New Zealand transfers 25 acres out of cotton and into wheat.

Realizing a Gain from Trade When One Country Has a Double Absolute Advantage

Stage 3: Countries trade

STAGE 3		
	New Zealand	*Australia*
	100 bushels (trade)	
Wheat	350 bushels	100 bushels
	(after trade)	
	200 bales (trade)	
Cotton	350 bales	100 bales
	(after trade)	

Gains from Comparative Advantage

- The real cost of producing cotton is the wheat that must be sacrificed to produce it.

- A country has a comparative advantage in cotton production if its opportunity cost, in terms of wheat, is lower than the other country.

Comparative Advantage
Means Lower Opportunity Cost

- Both Australia and New Zealand will gain when the terms of trade are set between 1:1 and 3:1, cotton to wheat.

Terms of Trade

- The ratio at which a country can trade domestic products for imported products is the *terms of trade*.

- The terms of trade determine how the gains from trade are distributed among trading partners.

Exchange Rates

- When trade is free—unimpeded by government-instituted barriers—patterns of trade and trade flows result from the independent decisions of thousands of importers and exporters and millions of private households and firms.

- To understand these patterns we must learn about exchange rates.

Exchange Rates

- An *exchange rate* is the ratio at which two currencies are traded, or the price of one currency in terms of another.

- For any pair of countries, there is a range of exchange rates that can lead automatically to both countries realizing the gains from specialization and comparative advantage.

© 2004 Prentice Hall Business Publishing   Principles of Microeconomics, 7/e   Karl Case, Ray Fair

---

Trade and Exchange Rates in a Two-Country/Two-Good World

- Exchange rates determine the terms of trade.

Domestic Prices of Timber (Per Foot) and Rolled Steel (Per Meter) in the United States and Brazil

	UNITED STATES	BRAZIL
Timber	$1	3 Reals
Rolled steel	$2	4 Reals

- The option of buying at home or importing will depend on the exchange rate.

© 2004 Prentice Hall Business Publishing   Principles of Microeconomics, 7/e   Karl Case, Ray Fair

---

Trade and Exchange Rates in a Two-Country/Two-Good World

Trade Flows Determined by Exchange Rates

EXCHANGE RATE	PRICE OF REAL	RESULT
$1 = 1 R	$1.00	Brazil imports timber and steel
$1 = 2 R	.50	Brazil imports timber
$1 = 2.1 R	.48	Brazil imports timber; United States imports steel
$1 = 2.9 R	.34	Brazil imports timber; United States imports steel
$1 = 3 R	.33	United States imports steel
$1 = 4 R	.25	United States imports timber and steel

© 2004 Prentice Hall Business Publishing   Principles of Microeconomics, 7/e   Karl Case, Ray Fair

Exchange Rates and Comparative Advantage

- If exchange rates end up in the right ranges, the free market will drive each country to shift resources into those sectors in which it enjoys a comparative advantage.

- Only those products in which a country has a comparative advantage will be competitive in world markets.

The Sources of Comparative Advantage

- *Factor endowments* refer to the quantity and quality of labor, land, and natural resources of a country.

- Factor endowments seem to explain a significant portion of actual world trade patterns.

The Heckscher-Ohlin Theorem

- The *Heckscher-Ohlin theorem* is a theory that explains the existence of a country's comparative advantage by its factor endowments.

- According to the theorem, a country has a comparative advantage in the production of a product if that country is relatively well endowed with inputs used intensively in the production of that product.

Other Explanations for Observed Trade Flows

- *Product differentiation* is a natural response to diverse preferences within an economy, and across economies.
- Some economists also distinguish between gains from *acquired comparative advantage* and gains from *natural comparative advantages*.

Other Explanations for Observed Trade Flows

- *Economies of scale* may be available when producing for a world market that would not be available when producing for a limited domestic market.

Trade Barriers: Tariffs, Export Subsidies, and Quotas

- **Protection** is the practice of shielding a sector of the economy from foreign competition.
- A *tariff* is a tax on imports.
- A *quota* is a limit on the quantity of imports.

Trade Barriers: Tariffs, Export Subsidies, and Quotas

- *Export subsidies* are government payments made to domestic firms to encourage exports.
- *Dumping* refers to a firm or industry that sells products on the world market at prices below the cost of production.

U.S. Trade Policies and GATT

- The *Smoot-Hawley tariff* was the U.S. tariff law of the 1930s, which set the highest tariff in U.S. history (60 percent). It set off an international trade war and caused the decline in trade that is often considered a cause of the worldwide depression of the 1930s.

U.S. Trade Policies and GATT

- The *General Agreement on Tariffs and Trade (GATT)* is an international agreement singed by the United States and 22 other countries in 1947 to promote the liberalization of foreign trade.

Economic Integration

- *Economic integration* occurs when two or more nations join to form a free-trade zone.

- The *European Union (EU)* and *the North American Free-Trade Agreement NAFTA* are examples of economic integration.

Economic Integration

- The *European Union (EU)* is the European trading bloc composed of Austria, Belgium, Denmark, Finland, France, Germany, Greece, Ireland, Italy, Luxembourg, the Netherlands, Portugal, Spain, Sweden, and the United Kingdom.

Economic Integration

- The *U.S.-Canadian Free-Trade Agreement* is an agreement in which the United States and Canada agreed to eliminate all barriers to trade between the two countries by 1988.

Economic Integration

- **The North American Free-Trade Agreement (NAFTA)** is an agreement signed by the United States, Mexico, and Canada in which the three countries agreed to establish all of North America as a free-trade zone.

The Case for Free Trade

- The case for free trade is based on the theory of comparative advantage. When countries specialize and trade based on comparative advantage, consumers pay less and consume more, and resources are used more efficiently.

- When tariffs and quotas are imposed, some of the gains from trade are lost.

The Gains from Trade

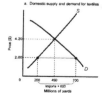

- When world price is $2, domestic quantity demanded rises, and quantity supplied falls. U.S. supply drops and resources are transferred to other sectors.

The Losses from the Imposition of a Tariff

a. Effect of $1 tariff per unit

- Government revenue equals the shaded area.

- The loss of efficiency from a $1 tariff:
  1. Consumers must pay a higher price for goods that could be produced at a lower cost.
  2. Marginal producers are drawn into textiles and away from other goods, resulting in inefficient domestic production.

© 2004 Prentice Hall Business Publishing   Principles of Microeconomics, 7/e   Karl Case, Ray Fair

The Case for Protection

- Protection saves jobs
- Some countries engage in unfair trade practices
- Cheap foreign labor makes competition unfair
- Protection safeguards national security
- Protection discourages dependency
- Protection safeguards infant industries

© 2004 Prentice Hall Business Publishing   Principles of Microeconomics, 7/e   Karl Case, Ray Fair

The Case for Protection

- An *infant industry* is a young industry that may need temporary protection from competition from the established industries of other countries to develop an acquired comparative advantage.

© 2004 Prentice Hall Business Publishing   Principles of Microeconomics, 7/e   Karl Case, Ray Fair

Review Terms and Concepts

absolute advantage	General Agreement on Tariffs and Trade (GATT)	Smoot-Hawley tariff
comparative advantage		tariff
Corn Laws	Heckscher-Ohlin theorem	terms of trade
dumping		theory of comparative advantage
economic integration	infant industry	
European Union (EU)	North American Free-Trade Agreement (NAFTA)	trade deficit
exchange rate		trade surplus
export subsidies	protection	U.S.-Canadian Free-Trade Agreement
factor endowments	quota	

© 2004 Prentice Hall Business Publishing   Principles of Microeconomics, 7/e   Karl Case, Ray Fair

---

CHAPTER 18

Globalization

Prepared by: Fernando Quijano
and Yvonn Quijano

© 2004 Prentice Hall Business Publishing   Principles of Microeconomics, 7/e   Karl Case, Ray Fair

---

Globalization

- **Globalization** is the process of increasing interdependence among countries and their citizens.

- **Economic globalization** is the process of increasing *economic* interdependence among countries and their citizens.

© 2004 Prentice Hall Business Publishing   Principles of Microeconomics, 7/e   Karl Case, Ray Fair

Economic Globalization: International Flows

© 2004 Prentice Hall Business Publishing   Principles of Microeconomics, 7/e   Karl Case, Ray Fair

The Global Circular Flow

- Opening the economy adds ten new flows:
    1. U.S. citizens buy foreign produced goods and services (imports).
    2. U.S. producers sell their goods and services abroad (exports).
    3. U.S. producers hire foreign workers.
    4. U.S. producers finance investment with foreign savings.

© 2004 Prentice Hall Business Publishing   Principles of Microeconomics, 7/e   Karl Case, Ray Fair

The Global Circular Flow

- Opening the economy adds ten new flows:
    5. U.S. citizens send saving abroad—buy foreign stocks and bonds, put money in foreign banks
    6. U.S. citizens supply labor to foreign companies or in foreign countries
    7. Foreign countries supply labor in the U.S. labor market

© 2004 Prentice Hall Business Publishing   Principles of Microeconomics, 7/e   Karl Case, Ray Fair

The Global Circular Flow

- Opening the economy adds ten new flows:

  8. Foreign citizens place savings in the U.S.—buy U.S. stocks and bonds, put money in U.S. banks

  9. Foreign producers hire workers in the U.S.

  10. Foreign producers finance investment with U.S. saving

The Global Circular Flow

- Efficiency in any economy, even the world economy, is achieved if capital and labor can move freely to where their productivity is the highest—where factors of production are put to wok in their "highest and best uses."

A Brief History of Economic Globalization

- Economic historian Jeffrey Williamson classifies the period of 1820-1914 as the first great period of globalization and the period since World War II as the second.

A Brief History of Economic Globalization

- Many dimensions of globalization are new today:
  - Sharp reductions in trade barriers
  - Increases in the flows of information and commerce over the Internet
  - Increased speed and lower cost of travel
  - Different nature of international relations.

The Free-Trade Debate Revisited

- The argument for free trade rests on two pieces of intuition:
  - Voluntary exchange is efficient, and
  - Comparative advantage. A country enjoys a *comparative advantage* in the production of a good if the production of that good has a lower opportunity cost than it would have if produced in another country.

The Free-Trade Debate Revisited

- Those who oppose trade make a number of arguments:
  - Buying imports simply ships jobs abroad
  - How can we compete with countries who pay low wages?
  - Free trade will hurt the environment.
  - The power of organizations like the WTO can undermine national sovereignty.

The Free-Trade Debate Revisited

- Proponents of free trade have a number of counter arguments:
  - We can't buy from countries unless they simultaneously buy from us. Exports to Mexico grew from $46 billion in 1995, just after NAFTA went into effect to $111 billion by 2000.

The Free-Trade Debate Revisited

- Proponents of free trade have a number of counter arguments:
  - Protecting an industry from foreign competition to save jobs will cost jobs in those sectors which would expand with free trade.
  - Protecting an industry can lead to inefficiency and a lack of ability to compete in world markets later on.

The Free-Trade Debate Revisited

- Proponents of free trade have a number of counter arguments:
  - Keeping the unemployment rate low is a macroeconomic issue. The correct tools for fighting unemployment are fiscal and monetary policies, not anti-trade policies.
  - If the objective is to reduce poverty, how can preventing trade help?

The Free-Trade Debate Revisited

- Proponents of free trade have a number of counter arguments:
  - The real hope for an improved environment is growth and responsible government. Feeding the citizenry comes first, and improving the environment comes later.

The Free-Trade Debate Revisited

- One final issue is the debate over *genetically modified (GM) foods* which are strains of food that have been genetically modified. Examples include insect and herbicide-resistant soybeans, corn, and cotton and rice with increased iron and vitamins.

Trade, Growth, and Poverty

- Controlling for other determinants of poverty and growth, is trade a plus or a minus?
  - Studies show that countries that were more integrated into the world economy grew faster than those that were less integrated.
  - When countries grow, the income of the lowest fifth of the income distribution rises at about the same rate as aggregate income.

The Globalization of Labor Markets: The Economics of Immigration

- The first "Great Migration" in the United States occurred between 1880 and 1924, when 25.8 million immigrants entered the country, a figure that represented 40% of the period's total population increase.

The Globalization of Labor Markets: The Economics of Immigration

- *The Immigration Reform and Control Act (1986)* granted amnesty to about 3 million illegal aliens and imposed a strong set of employer sanctions designed to slow the flow of immigrants into the United States.

- *The Immigration Act of 1990* increased the number of legal immigrants allowed into the United States each year by 150,000.

The Globalization of Labor Markets: The Economics of Immigration

IMMIGRANTS INTO THE UNITED STATES BY COUNTRY OF ORIGIN, 1991-2000

RANK	COUNTRY	THOUSANDS OF IMMIGRANTS	RANK	COUNTRY	THOUSANDS OF IMMIGRANTS
1	Mexico	2,251	8	Haiti	182
2	Philippines	506	9	Cuba	181
3	China	425	10	Jamaica	174
4	Vietnam	421	11	South Korea	172
5	India	383	12	Poland	170
6	Dominican Republic	341	13	Ukraine	142
7	El Salvador	218	14	Canada	138

Economic Arguments
for Free Immigration

- Free immigration increases world output.
  - If the productivity of low-wage workers is higher in the United States than in Mexico, the same labor force produces more total output after immigration, and world output rises.

Economic Arguments
for Free Immigration

- Free immigration increases world output.
  - Immigrants do not necessarily displace U.S. workers but rather take jobs that Americans simply do not want.
  - Almost all U.S. citizens except Native Americans have recent ancestors who came to this country as immigrants.

The Argument
Against Free Immigration

- The distribution of income is likely to change in response to immigration, affecting the returns to both labor and capital.
- Immigrants take jobs away from low-income Americans and drive up unemployment rates.
- Immigrants end up on welfare rolls and become a burden to taxpayers.

The Evidence:
The Net Costs of Immigration

- David Card of Berkeley looked at the impact of the large inflow of Cuban immigrants in 1980 on wages and unemployment in the Miami area.

- He found virtually no effect.

- Other studies suggest that low-skilled immigrants caused one third of the drop in the wages of high-school dropouts.

The Evidence:
The Net Costs of Immigration

- First-generation immigrants as a whole might be paying more in taxes than they collect in means-tested benefits such as welfare.

- But there has been a dramatic drop in the level of education, experience, and skills among immigrants. They contribute less in tax revenues than the amount they collect in benefits.

Capital Mobility

- The argument for free and open financial market mobility is that capital should flow to its highest and best use.

Capital Mobility

- To reduce the volatility of capital flows to emerging-market countries, countries can shut themselves from international capital flows.

- But the revealed preference of these countries is to stay involved with the international financial system.

Public Policy and Globalization

- Other policy debates beyond the issues of free trade and free mobility of resources include:
  - Global public goods, or externalities
  - The impact of non-governmental organizations (NGO's) on world growth, and their powerful roles in enforcing international monetary agreements and trade rules.

Global Externalities and Public Goods

- **Public goods**, sometimes called **social goods**, are goods or services that bestow collective benefits on members of society.

- Taking action to slow global warming presumably would produce a worldwide public good. Since no nation can be excluded, and the impact on a single nation is small, there is no incentive to contribute.

Global Externalities and Public Goods

- An *externality* is a cost or a benefit resulting from some activity or transaction that is imposed or bestowed on some party outside the activity or transaction.

- One of the functions of government is to "internalize" externalities with something like a pollution tax.

Global Externalities and Public Goods

- If the number of countries is small, bargaining and negotiation may resolve the issue. But where large numbers of jurisdictions are involved, the public goods' problems arise.

Nongovernmental Organizations and International Economics: The Washington Consensus

- While there is considerable disagreement about who formed it or how strongly it was designed to be enforced, a set of objectives or goals were laid down for countries that the IMF was financing.

- What came to be referred to as the "*Washington Consensus*" had ten elements.

Nongovernmental Organizations and International
Economics: The Washington Consensus

1. Fiscal discipline—modest budget
deficits or balanced budget,

2. public expenditure priorities in health
and education,

3. tax reform—the tax base should be
broad and marginal tax rates should be
low,

4. positive but moderate market-
determined interest rates,

Nongovernmental Organizations and International
Economics: The Washington Consensus

5. a competitive—ideally floating—
exchange rate as the "first essential
element of an outward-oriented
economic policy,

6. import liberalization—essentially a free
trade policy for reduced tariffs,

7. openness to foreign investment,

Nongovernmental Organizations and International
Economics: The Washington Consensus

8. privatization—"based on the idea that
private industry is managed more
efficiently than public enterprises."

9. deregulation, and

10. protection of property rights.

• Clearly, considerable disagreement
existed about the degree to which
these elements should or could be
enforced. A new consensus has
emerged for gradualism.

Globalization, Capitalism, and Democracy

- Advocates of globalization often are staunch supporters of laissez faire capitalism.

- But the issue of openness and the desirability of interdependence between national economies probably does not depend on the kind of economic or political system that a country chooses to establish.

Globalization, Capitalism, and Democracy

- The terms democracy and dictatorship refer to the institutions of government and to the process of public choice.

- The terms socialism and capitalism refer, on the other hand, to the economic institutions that determine the allocation of resources.

Globalization, Capitalism, and Democracy

- A pure socialist economy is one in which the government owns the land and capital and in which resources are allocated essentially by a central government plan.

- A laissez faire capitalist economy is one in which the government plays virtually no role in directing the economy.

Globalization, Capitalism, and Democracy

- The debate is really not about government vs. no government. It is instead about the role of government in the economy in addition to:
  - Providing public goods
  - Regulating monopoly power
  - Internalizing external costs and benefits
  - Ensuring that all economic agents are well informed

Globalization, Capitalism, and Democracy

- More debatable issues about the role of government in the economy include:
  - Government involvement in income redistribution, and
  - The potential role of government in stabilizing the economy.
- Economists as a whole tend to favor globalization, but there is a wide range of opinion on the proper role of government in the economy.

A Final Word

- A powerful logic exists in support of economic openness:
  - The free flow of resources and goods and services across national borders, driven by efficient economic incentives, including the desire to maximize profit, is likely to make citizens better off than if borders were closed and economies turned inward.

Review Terms and Concepts

comparative advantage

economic globalization

externality

genetically modified (GM) foods

globalization

The Immigration Act of 1990

The Immigration Reform and Control Act (1986)

public goods, or social goods

Washington Consensus

CHAPTER **19**

Economic Growth in Developing and Transitional Economies

Prepared by: Fernando Quijano
and Yvonn Quijano

Economic Growth in Developing and Transitional Economies

- The universality of scarcity makes economic analysis relevant to all nations.

- Economic problems and policy instruments are different, but economic thinking about these problems can be transferred easily from country to country.

Life in the Developing Nations: Population and Poverty

- The United States and other industrialized economies rarely face the difficulties faced by developing nations:
  - chronic food shortages
  - explosive population growth
  - hyperinflations
  - low productivity and low GDP per capita
  - primitive shelter
  - illiteracy
  - infant mortality

Life in the Developing Nations: Population and Poverty

Indicators of Economic Development

COUNTRY GROUP	POPULATION (MILLIONS) 2002	GROSS NATIONAL INCOME PER CAPITA, 2002 (DOLLARS)	ANNUAL HEALTH EXPENDITURES PER CAPITA 2001 (DOLLARS)	INFANT MORTALITY, 2001 (DEATHS BEFORE AGE FIVE PER 1,000 BIRTHS)	PERCENTAGE OF POPULATION IN URBAN AREAS, 2001
Low-income (e.g., China, Ethiopia, Haiti, India)	2,495	430	21.5	121.7	32
Lower middle-income (e.g., Guatemala, Poland, Philippines, Thailand)	2,411	1,390	72.3	42.2	42
Upper middle-income (e.g., Brazil, Malaysia, Mexico)	331	5,040	308.9	28.6	76
Industrial market economies (e.g., Japan, Germany, New Zealand, United States)	965	26,310	2,736	7.1	79

Source: World Bank, WWW.WORLDBANK.ORG

Life in the Developing Nations: Population and Poverty

- In the year 2,002, the world population reached over 6.2 billion people. Most of the world's more than 200 nations belong to the developing world.

- While the developed nations account for only about one-quarter of the world's population, they consume about three-quarters of the world's output.

- Developing countries have three-fourths of the world's population, but only one-fourth of the world's income.

Economic Development: Sources and Strategies

- Almost all developing nations have a scarcity of physical capital relative to other resources, especially labor.
  - The *vicious-circle-of-poverty hypothesis* suggests that poverty is self-perpetuating because poor nations are unable to save and invest enough to accumulate the capital stock that would help them grow.
    - Poverty alone cannot explain capital shortages, and poverty is not necessarily self-perpetuating.

The Sources of Economic Development

- *Capital flight* is the tendency for both human capital and financial capital to leave developing countries in search of higher rates of return elsewhere.
  - Price ceilings, import controls, and expropriation are some of the policies that discourage investment.
  - The absence of productive capital prevents income from rising.

The Sources of Economic Development

- Just as financial capital seeks the highest return, so does human capital:
  - *Brain drain* is the tendency for talented people from developing countries to become educated in a developed country and remain there after graduation.
    - Development cannot proceed without human resources capable of initiating and managing economic activity.

The Sources of Economic Development

- *Social overhead capital* is the basic infrastructure projects such as roads, power generation, and irrigation systems that add to a nation's productive capacity.

  - In developing economies, government provision of public goods is highly deficient, and many socially useful projects cannot be successfully undertaken by the private sector.

© 2004 Prentice Hall Business Publishing   Principles of Microeconomics, 7/e   Karl Case, Ray Fair

Strategies for Economic Development

- A developing economy with insufficient human and physical capital faces some very basic trade-offs. Three of these trade-offs are:

  - Agriculture versus industry.

  - Exports versus import substitution.

  - Central planning versus the market.

© 2004 Prentice Hall Business Publishing   Principles of Microeconomics, 7/e   Karl Case, Ray Fair

Agriculture or Industry?

- Industry has some apparent attractions over agriculture:

  - The building of factories is an important step toward increasing the stock of capital.

  - Developed economies have experienced a structural transition from agriculture to industrialization and greater provision of services.

- However, industrialization in many developed countries has not brought the benefits that were expected.

© 2004 Prentice Hall Business Publishing   Principles of Microeconomics, 7/e   Karl Case, Ray Fair

Agriculture or Industry?

The Structure of Production in Selected Developed and Developing Economies, 2001

COUNTRY	PER CAPITA GROSS NATIONAL INCOME (GNI)	PERCENTAGE OF GROSS DOMESTIC PRODUCT		
		AGRICULTURE	INDUSTRY	SERVICES
Tanzania	$ 270	45	16	39
Bangladesh	360	23	25	52
China	840	15	57	34
Thailand	1,440	10	41	49
Colombia	1,890	13	30	57
Brazil	3,070	9	34	57
Korea	9,460	4	42	54
United States	34,280	2	25	73
Japan	35,610	1	32	67

Source: World Bank, WWW.WORLDBANK.ORG, 2003.

© 2004 Prentice Hall Business Publishing   Principles of Microeconomics, 7/e   Karl Case, Ray Fair

Exports or Import Substitution?

- **Import substitution** is an industrial trade strategy that favors developing local industries that can manufacture goods to replace imports.

© 2004 Prentice Hall Business Publishing   Principles of Microeconomics, 7/e   Karl Case, Ray Fair

Exports or Import Substitution?

- The import-substitution strategy has failed almost everywhere for the following reasons:
  - Domestic industries, sheltered from international competition, develop major economic inefficiencies.
  - Import substitution encouraged the production of capital-intensive production methods, which limited the creation of jobs.
  - The cost of the resulting output was far greater than the price of that output in world markets.

© 2004 Prentice Hall Business Publishing   Principles of Microeconomics, 7/e   Karl Case, Ray Fair

Exports or Import Substitution?

- *Export promotion* is a trade policy designed to encourage exports.
  - Several countries including Japan, the "four little dragons," Brazil, Colombia, and Turkey, have had some success with outward-looking trade policy.
  - Government policies to promote exports include subsidies to export industries and the maintenance of a favorable exchange rate environment.

© 2004 Prentice Hall Business Publishing   Principles of Microeconomics, 7/e   Karl Case, Ray Fair

Central Planning or the Market?

- Today, planning takes many forms in developing nations.
- The economic appeal of planning lies in its ability to channel savings into productive investment and to coordinate economic activities that otherwise might not exist.
- The reality of central planning is that it is technically difficult, highly politicized, and difficult to administer.

© 2004 Prentice Hall Business Publishing   Principles of Microeconomics, 7/e   Karl Case, Ray Fair

Central Planning or the Market?

- Market-oriented reforms recommended by international agencies include:
  - the elimination of price controls,
  - privatization of state-run enterprises, and
  - reductions in import restraints.

© 2004 Prentice Hall Business Publishing   Principles of Microeconomics, 7/e   Karl Case, Ray Fair

Central Planning or the Market?

- The *International Monetary Fund* is an international agency whose primary goals are to stabilize international exchange rates and to lend money to countries that have problems financing their international transactions.

Central Planning or the Market?

- The *World Bank* is an international agency that lends money to individual countries for projects that promote economic development.

Growth Versus Development: The Policy Cycle

- *Structural adjustment* is a series of programs in developing nations designed to:
  1. reduce the size of their public sectors through privatization and/or expenditure reductions,
  2. decrease their budget deficits,
  3. control inflation, and
  4. encourage private saving and investment through tax reform.

Issues in Economic Development

- The growth of the population in developing nations is about 1.7 percent per year, compared to only 0.5 percent per year in industrial market economies.

- Thomas Malthus, England's first professor of political economy, believed populations grow geometrically. He believed that due to the diminished marginal productivity of land, food supplies grow much more slowly.

© 2004 Prentice Hall Business Publishing   Principles of Microeconomics, 7/e   Karl Case, Ray Fair

---

The Growth of World Population, Projected to 2020 A.D.

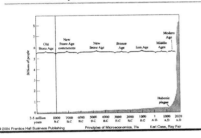

© 2004 Prentice Hall Business Publishing   Principles of Microeconomics, 7/e   Karl Case, Ray Fair

---

Population Growth

- Population growth is determined by the relationship between births and deaths.

- The *fertility rate*, or birth rate, equals:

$$\frac{\text{number of births per year}}{\text{population}} \times 100$$

- The *mortality rate*, or death rate, equals:

$$\frac{\text{number of deaths per year}}{\text{population}} \times 100$$

© 2004 Prentice Hall Business Publishing   Principles of Microeconomics, 7/e   Karl Case, Ray Fair

Population Growth

- The *natural rate of population increase* is the difference between the birth rate and the death rate. It does not take migration into account.

- Any nation that wants to slow its rate of population growth will probably find it necessary to have in place economic incentives for fewer children as well as family planning programs.

Developing-Country Debt Burdens

- *Debt rescheduling* is an agreement between banks and borrowers through which a new schedule of repayments of the debt is negotiated; often some of the debt is written off and the repayment period is extended.

- A *stabilization program* is an agreement between a borrower country and the International Monetary Fund in which the country agrees to revamp its economic policies to provide incentives for higher export earnings and lower imports.

Political Systems and Economic Systems: Socialism, Capitalism, and Communism

- *Democracy* and *dictatorship* refer to *political* systems.

  - A *democracy* is a system of government in which ultimate power rests with the people, who make governmental decisions either directly through voting or indirectly through representatives.

  - A *dictatorship* is a political system in which ultimate power is concentrated in either a small elite group or a single person.

Political Systems and Economic Systems:
Socialism, Capitalism, and Communism

- Two major *economic* systems have
  existed: socialism and capitalism.

  - A *socialist economy* is one in which
    most capital—factories, equipment,
    buildings, railroads, and so forth—is
    owned by the government rather than
    by private citizens. *Social ownership* is
    another term that is used to describe a
    socialist economy.

Political Systems and Economic Systems:
Socialism, Capitalism, and Communism

- Two major *economic* systems have
  existed: socialism and capitalism.

  - A *capitalist economy* is one in which
    most capital is privately owned.

Political Systems and Economic Systems:
Socialism, Capitalism, and Communism

- *Communism* is an economic system
  in which the people control the
  means of production (capital and
  land) directly, without the
  intervention of a government or
  state.

Political Systems and Economic Systems: Socialism, Capitalism, and Communism

- Comparing economies today, the real distinction is between centrally planned socialism and capitalism, not between capitalism and communism.

- No pure socialist economies and no pure capitalist economies exist.

- The United States supports many government enterprises, including the postal system, although public ownership is the exception.

© 2004 Prentice Hall Business Publishing   Principles of Microeconomics, 7/e   Karl Case, Ray Fair

Political Systems and Economic Systems: Socialism, Capitalism, and Communism

- Whether particular kinds of political systems tend to be associated with particular kinds of economic systems is debatable.

- There are capitalist economies with democratic political institutions; socialist economies that maintain strong democratic traditions; and democratic countries with strong socialist institutions.

- At the heart of both the market system *and* democracy is individual freedom.

© 2004 Prentice Hall Business Publishing   Principles of Microeconomics, 7/e   Karl Case, Ray Fair

Central Planning Versus the Market

- Just as there are no pure capitalist and no pure socialist economies, there are no pure market economies and no pure planned economies.

- A *market-socialist economy* is an economy that combines government ownership with market allocation.

© 2004 Prentice Hall Business Publishing   Principles of Microeconomics, 7/e   Karl Case, Ray Fair

The Transition to a Market Economy

- Economists generally agree on six basic requirements for a successful transition from socialism to a market-based system:

  1. macroeconomic stabilization;

  2. deregulation of prices and liberalization of trade;

  3. privatization of state-owned enterprises and development of new private industry;

The Transition to a Market Economy

- Economists generally agree on six basic requirements for a successful transition from socialism to a market-based system:

  4. the establishment of market-supporting institutions, such as property and contract laws, accounting systems, and so forth;

  5. a social safety net to deal with unemployment and poverty; and

  6. external assistance.

The Transition to a Market Economy

- The *tragedy of commons* is the idea that collective ownership may not provide the proper private incentives for efficiency because individuals do not bear the full costs of their own decisions but do enjoy the full benefits.

The Transition to a Market Economy

- **Shock therapy** is the approach to transition from socialism to market capitalism that advocates rapid deregulation of prices, liberalization of trade, and privatization.

- Advocates of a *gradualist* approach believe that the best course of action is to build up market institutions first, gradually decontrol prices, and privatize only the most efficient government enterprises.

© 2004 Prentice Hall Business Publishing   Principles of Microeconomics, 7/e   Karl Case, Ray Fair

Review Terms and Concepts

brain drain

capital flight

capitalist economy

communism

debt rescheduling

export promotion

fertility rate

import substitution

International Monetary Fund, IMF

market-socialist economy

mortality rate

natural rate of population increase

shock therapy

social overhead capital

socialist economy

stabilization program

structural adjustment

tragedy of commons

vicious-circle-of-poverty hypothesis

World Bank

© 2004 Prentice Hall Business Publishing   Principles of Microeconomics, 7/e   Karl Case, Ray Fair